QUICK ESCAPES® FROM
Dallas/Fort Worth

The Best Weekend Getaways

SEVENTH EDITION

June Naylor

travel

Guilford, Connecticut

To buy books in quantity for corporate use
or incentives, call **(800) 962-0973**
or e-mail **premiums@GlobePequot.com**.

Editor: Amy Lyons
Project Editor: Heather Santiago
Layout: Melissa Evarts
Text design: Sheryl P. Kober
Maps: Design Maps Inc. © Morris Book Publishing, LLC.

ISSN 1540-4374
ISBN 978-0-7627-6042-8

Printed in the United States of America
10 9 8 7 6 5 4 3 2 1

For Max—with anticipation of our many adventures in our great state of Texas

ABOUT THE AUTHOR

A sixth-generation Texan and Fort Worth native, **June Naylor** has written for the *Fort Worth Star-Telegram* (a McClatchy newspaper) since 1984, starting in sports and writing for the state and metro desks before moving to the travel section to write stories about Texas, the Southwest, the United States, and the world. She added food and dining to the mix in 1987 and currently writes about dining, food, and travel for the *Star-Telegram* features section. A contributor to numerous magazines, June is the coauthor with noted cowboy cook Grady Spears of *The Texas Cowboy Kitchen.*

The author of Globe Pequot's *Insiders' Guide to Dallas & Fort Worth* and *Texas Off the Beaten Path,* June has received several writing and photography awards from the Society of American Travel Writers and the Association of Women Journalists.

ACKNOWLEDGMENTS

Efforts like this book remain a joy to me, but they're usually a tremendous challenge for those around me. I truly love the research and hours of writing—which spread into endless nights and weekends—because traveling in Texas is an absolute passion of mine. There are countless hours and times in which I pushed everyone dear to me away so I could work. I have only deep thanks for those who endured, including my loving parents and extraordinary family and my ever-patient friends. And I owe much gratitude for the hard work and keen eye provided also by Lauren Rausch. May you find much happiness in writing about travel.

CONTENTS

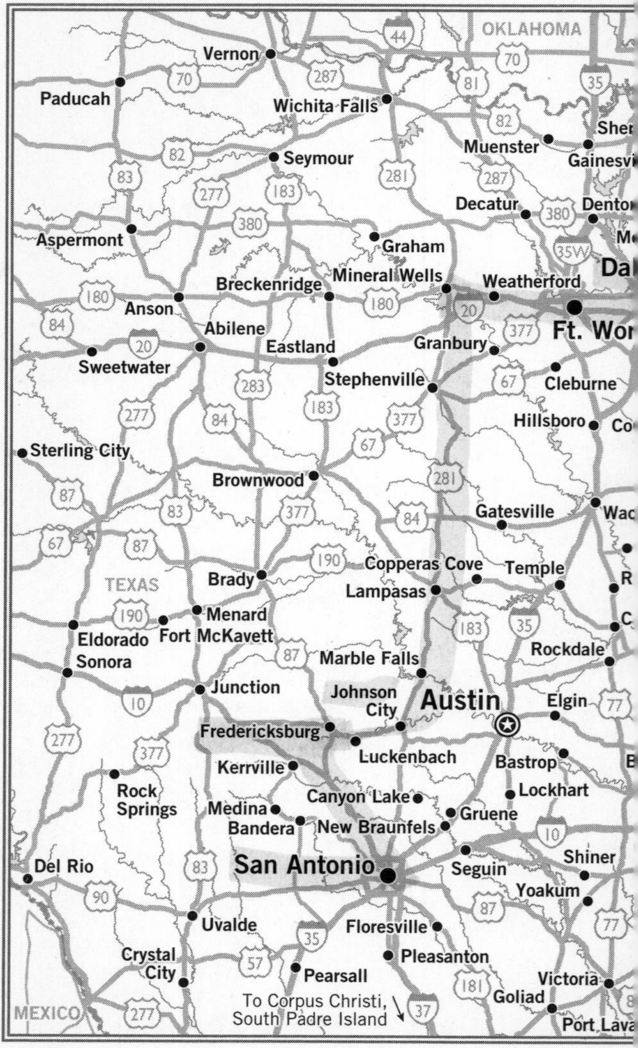

OKLAHOMA
Vernon
Paducah
Wichita Falls
Muenster
Gainesvi
Sher
Seymour
Decatur
Dento
Aspermont
Graham
Breckenridge
Mineral Wells
Weatherford
Da
Anson
Abilene
Ft. Wor
Eastland
Granbury
Sweetwater
Stephenville
Cleburne
Hillsboro
Sterling City
Brownwood
Gatesville
Wac
TEXAS
Brady
Copperas Cove
Temple
Lampasas
Menard
Eldorado
Fort McKavett
Sonora
Marble Falls
Rockdale
Junction
Johnson City
Austin
Elgin
Fredericksburg
Luckenbach
Bastrop
Kerrville
Rock Springs
Medina
Canyon Lake
Lockhart
Bandera
New Braunfels
Gruene
San Antonio
Seguin
Shiner
Del Rio
Yoakum
Uvalde
Floresville
Crystal City
Pleasanton
Pearsall
Victoria
Goliad
To Corpus Christi, South Padre Island
MEXICO
Port Lava
44
70
287
81
35
82
83
277
183
281
380
35W
180
20
377
84
283
67
87
190
10
77
90
57
181
37

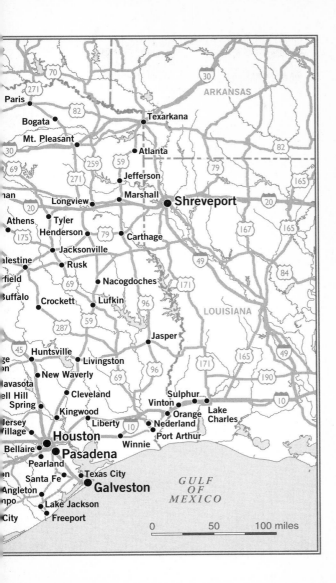

INTRODUCTION

When pioneers in the 1800s made their way westward to settle in the plains of north Texas, many eventually chose to put roots down on the banks of the Trinity River branches that flow through what are now the sprawling cities of Dallas and Fort Worth. Most stayed put, building lives in ranching and trading around these villages, needing to journey no more.

Both of these burgs grew rapidly and haven't stopped since. Dallas's banking, retail, and high-tech industries have been nothing short of explosive, while Fort Worth's airline, manufacturing, and Western heritage businesses continue to thrive. Although each bears a distinctly separate personality, the two cities have spread so dramatically that what was once a 30-mile distance between them no longer exists. Major highways, suburbs, amusement parks, and shopping malls have so completely filled the gap that the two, with a combined population of about five million, are simply called the Metroplex.

Certainly the Metroplex has much to offer in terms of leisure activities, but it is the act of wandering and exploring smaller, simpler places that restores the soul. Southbound getaways, for instance, are filled with the Victorian splendors of Galveston or Waxahachie, the sandy solace of Port Aransas, or the German heritage and charming bed-and-breakfast hideaways of the Hill Country. Escaping eastbound means delving into the woodsy retreats and antiques hamlets of Jefferson or Marshall, while westbound wanderings lead to history-rich towns such as Glen Rose and Albany.

Northward there are the lakes and hills found in Oklahoma, the horse country around Denton, and yet more German history around Muenster. For anyone needing still more diversion, there are surprisingly easy escapes to the sands at South Padre Island.

Taking such breaks from city life is incomparably therapeutic. Making an escape—for a couple of days or a weekend—from daily stress, commuting, yard work, or deadlines is usually what makes us able to best deal with everyday stress.

With that in mind, these itineraries were designed to provide all the necessary information for truly getting away. Herein, find a mix of driving trips, among others, that give you the option of hopping on an hourlong flight that will keep your travel time within a true Quick Escape definition. In every case, you'll find the tours complete with descriptions of destinations, attractions, activities, restaurants, and lodgings. For every tour there are listings such as **Special Events, Other Recommended Restaurants and Lodgings,** and **There's More,** which describes additional attractions in the area. For even more background, maps, guides, specific dates of certain events, and other details, you can contact the local visitor offices that are listed under **For More Information** at the end of each chapter.

If you can, plan your trip ahead of time. Although there's nothing more fun than escaping on a whim, a retreat is often more relaxing if you know where you'll sleep at night. If you don't have time to call all sorts of places, consult an expert.

If you yearn for Texas places steeped in history, where feather comforters and pillows help ease away your city-life stress, consult the group called the **Texas Bed and Breakfast Association.** This outfit grants membership after strict inspections and defines its members in clear terms. Room rates, children restrictions, smoking allowances, and such are always described in the listings, which give a clear idea of what you're paying for, up front. Contact the organization at (800) 428-0368. Visit the Web site for full descriptions of properties at www.texasbb.org. Most restaurants and lodgings suggested are in a moderate price range, while just a few more expensive, special places are included when warranted. Rates and prices are not included, as these can often change without notice.

Do think ahead when making an escape to avoid peak traffic times on the Dallas and Fort Worth freeways. Outbound routes from Dallas are particularly clogged by 4 p.m. on weekdays, and the freeways between Dallas and Fort Worth are always jammed during morning and afternoon rush hours.

Please note that when traveling south or north from Dallas and Fort Worth, I-35 is often the general label for the interstate. The highway courses all the way from the Mexican border across the Oklahoma state line, splitting into two interstates for use in both halves of the Metroplex; in Dallas, it's I-35E, and in Fort Worth, I-35W. The two rejoin north of the Metroplex in Denton and south in Hillsboro as I-35. No matter which you take, you'll wind up at your destination.

For maximum enjoyment of your trips, it's wise to take along some necessities, including sunblock and hat, insect repellent, comfortable walking shoes, picnic basket or daypack, camera, and bottled water. And although maps are provided here for general locations, you should pick up more detailed maps whenever possible.

For more information, including free maps and guides, contact the **Texas Department of Transportation, Travel and Information Division,** P.O. Box 5064, Austin, TX 78763-5064; (800) 452-9292; and the **Tourism Division, Texas Department of Commerce,** P.O. Box 12728, Austin, TX 78711; (800) 888-8TEX. Visit the state tourism Web site at www.traveltex.com.

SOUTHBOUND ESCAPES

SOUTHBOUND ESCAPE *One*
Houston and Galveston (By Plane)
FROM BIG CITY TO CLASSIC BEACH/2 NIGHTS

- World-class museums
- Revitalized downtown
- Exceptional dining
- Victorian heritage
- Beaches and rain forest
- Outer space

In Texas's younger years, Galveston was the port through which seafaring arrivals to the frontier entered, and it was one of the nation's busiest, too. But with the construction of the Houston Ship Channel and the first steamship's passage up the Buffalo Bayou to the city of Houston in 1837, Houston's relationship with the Gulf of Mexico and international shipping changed dramatically. Now the fourth-largest city in the country, Houston's immediate connection with the ocean adds to its global significance.

The energy industry finds a happy home in Houston, too, as does the nation's space program. But Houston's not all about heavy industry, by any means: Some of the world's finest art can be viewed in Houston, and it's the place where serious shoppers can find original fashion and home design. The culinary scene has become a driving force in H-town, and you can often count on finding celebrities, such as Houston native Beyoncé, out on the town.

Less than an hour south, Galveston was known—during its mid-19th-century heyday—as the Wall Street of the Southwest. Cotton was king, and this was a tremendously wealthy city. Prospering on the Gulf of Mexico, as did New Orleans, Galveston ruled this part of the coast for many years.

Today Galveston, home to about 58,000 residents, is filled with wonderful vestiges of its Victorian past. Get away from home and delve into a rich history of Italianate mansions and gingerbread

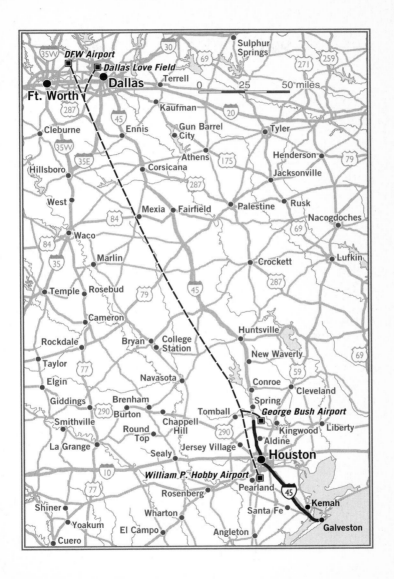

houses, and see how miraculously the city was rebuilt after the devastating hurricane of 1900.

DAY 1/MORNING

The only way to make this trip a Quick Escape is by hopping a plane for Houston. From DFW Airport, you can board a plane to **George Bush Intercontinental Airport;** or from Dallas Love Field, you'll catch a plane for **William P. Hobby Airport.** Either way, the flight is less than an hour in length, and you'll pick up a rental car (all major companies are represented at the airports) to get around. Pick up a bagel or granola bar at the airport to tide you over until lunch.

Upon arrival in Houston, head to the **Museum District,** home to seventeen separate museums and cultural centers, immediately southwest of downtown (Bissonnet at Montrose, with Hermann Park to the south; www.houstonmuseumdistrict.org).

Highlights there include **The Museum of Fine Arts, Houston** (www.mfah.org), where 57,000 works are housed within more than 300,000 square feet of exhibition space, including several buildings and gardens; the **Menil Collection** (www.menil.org), an extraordinary assemblage of 20th-century art, with some 15,000 paintings, sculptures, prints, drawings, photographs, and rare books among the pieces to see; the **Holocaust Museum Houston** (www.hmh.org), which includes among its permanent exhibits 30-minute films sharing the experiences of Houston-area residents who lived through the Holocaust; and the **Children's Museum of Houston** (www.cmhouston.org), recently expanded to offer 90,000 square feet of exhibits and activities for kids.

If you want to do the best possible whirlwind tour of Houston, it's pretty much a snap with **City Pass Houston,** which covers six attractions at a savings of nearly 50 percent overall. The ticket costs $39 for adults and $29 for children 4 to 11, and includes admissions to **Space Center Houston, the Downtown Aquarium, the Houston Museum of Natural Science,** and the **Houston Zoo.** You can also choose between the Museum of Fine Arts or The Children's Museum and the **George Ranch Historical Park or The Health Museum.** Go online to purchase this pass in advance (www.visit houstontexas.com and at www.citypass.com).

LUNCH Keeping it casual in the Museum District means digging into custom tacos at **Bodega's Taco Shop** 1200 Binz St. (www.bodegastacoshop .com), where you have choices such as rotisserie chicken, ground sirloin, or fajita steak fillings and more than ten flavors of salsa. Or you can hit a retro diner called **Little Big's** inside Hermann Park (1600 Zoo Circle Dr.; http://littlebigshouston.com /LittleBurgersBigTaste.htm), where the menu offers sliders (mini-burgers) with fries and shakes.

AFTERNOON

Head downtown where **Discovery Green** makes it fun to go outside and play again. This twelve-acre park sitting smack in the middle of downtown (1500 McKinney St.; www.discoverygreen.com) opened in 2008, replacing parking lots that faced the George R. Brown Convention Center. A perimeter of century-old live oaks provide a natural framework within which designers built an expanse that includes the Great Lawn, grand-scale pieces of art, a big pond for boating, green spaces occupied by a giant fountain (fun for kids to splash in during hot days), dog fountains and runs, picnic grounds, playgrounds, an amphitheater, jogging trails, and places to play bocce ball, horseshoes, and croquet. The $122 million project includes restaurants such as **The Grove,** a Robert Del Grande operation serving American rustic cuisine with lots of rotisserie specialties; the **Treehouse,** a super-casual drinks and snacks place; and the **Lake House,** a fast-casual spot serving burgers, hot dogs, salads, shakes, wine, and beer.

Green is a keyword at Discovery Green, as all concessions are eco-friendly, utilizing all-biodegradable products. A full schedule of performing arts includes opera, blues, jazz, and ballet on various stages, and monthly offerings include authors' readings, ballroom dance lessons, Pilates and yoga classes, and kids' writing workshops.

For more outdoor exploration at the heart of the city, visit **Sam Houston Park,** sitting in the shadows of downtown's high-rises, which offers guided tours of historic homes in the park (www.her itagesociety.org), and hiking and biking trails that wind through downtown along **Buffalo Bayou** (www.buffalobayou.org).

DINNER   **The Grove** (downtown at 1611 Lamar St.; http://thegrove houston.com) is Discovery Green's showcase restaurant. An original concept from Houston's foremost celebrity chef, Robert Del Grande, this destination dining spot features American rustic cuisine that includes free-range deviled eggs with Spanish chorizo and tapenade, and braised long island duck legs with baby turnips and wild mushrooms. The setting brings the outdoors in, too, with woods and natural fibers, plus artwork fashioned after nature.

NIGHTLIFE   Stay downtown to enjoy the bounty of hot spots within the **Houston Pavilions** (1201 Fannin St.; www.houstonpavilions.com). This complex houses Lucky Strike, House of Blues, Pete's Dueling Piano Bar, Red Cat Jazz Café, and Cork Wine Bar.

LODGING   You'll kick back in style at the elegant **Four Seasons** (1300 Lamar St.; 713-650-1300; www.fourseasons.com/houston), a 25-year-old beauty that's been superbly renovated. Sitting across from Discovery Green, the hotel offers a magnificent new pool deck, where a $4 million overhaul delivers a truly sublime resort experience in the middle of downtown. Brazilian woods, Turkish travertine flooring, iridescent colored tiles, fire pit, and curvy lines provide a sexy framework for the saltwater pool, as well as bar and cafe areas.

DAY 2/MORNING

BREAKFAST Enjoy a luxurious breakfast at the Four Seasons, then check out, hop in your car, and head south toward Galveston.

En route to the beach, stop for a morning tour at **Space Center Houston** in the area called Clear Lake (1601 NASA Parkway; www .spacecenter.org). There, you can explore the **Johnson Space Center,** home to the renowned NASA program. You'll see a mixture of museum exhibits—including space suits and scale models of lunar equipment—with hands-on areas for kids and adults. A 90-minute tram tour takes guests onto JSC grounds and into buildings, such as the one housing the historic mission control and another containing a life-size mock-up of the International Space Station. Visitors can't help but note open green spaces where trees have been planted in memory of the astronauts who lost their lives in service.

If you plan ahead and allow plenty of time, you can take advantage of the **Level 9 Tour** (it's an $85 ticket), which includes a hot lunch in the JSC cafeteria, where astronauts eat. You'll see abundant behind-the-scenes areas at the space center. Tickets must be purchased in advance (at www.spacecenter.org) and are available to visitors age 14 and older. Only twelve guests at a time may take the daily tour. Note that the tour lasts 4½ to 5 hours and that cancellations less than two days in advance are nonrefundable.

LUNCH Less than five minutes from SCH, the lunch spot of choice is **Frenchie's** (1041 NASA Parkway; 281-486-7144), a friendly joint with side-splitting dishes that include fettuccine Alfredo, pasta primavera, and excellent eggplant parmesan. The main attraction, however, is the decor, consisting of wall-to-wall autographed astronaut photos and hundreds of pieces of NASA memorabilia.

AFTERNOON

Head south to Galveston and directly to the center of the island town, now officially called the **Historic Downtown, Strand and Seaport,** the waterfront area designated a National Historic Landmark District. Here, find one of the nation's largest collections of restored Victorian buildings, transformed into a colorful mercantile center located within the old wharfside business zone. The former banking buildings and cotton warehouses along the district now house a trove of antiques and jazz music possibilities. Hurricane Ike whipped through the area in devastating fashion in 2008, but as has been its custom, Galveston has made an admirable rebound.

There's no better orientation for the Galveston visitor than seeing the *Great Storm* at Pier 21, 2016 Strand (409-763-8808). You'll gain a deep appreciation for the early residents' nightmare that was the devastating 1900 hurricane by watching the wide-screen multiimage presentation. The story of how some 6,000 people died is told in photographs, eyewitness accounts, and dramatic sound and light effects. Shows on the hour daily 11 a.m. to 6 p.m. and until 8 p.m. Fri and Sat. Admission is $4 for adults, students 7 to 18 $3, children 6 and under are free.

The centerpiece of the Strand and the Texas Seaport Museum is the *ELISSA,* Texas's tall ship and another National Historic Landmark, as well as a designated treasure by the National Trust for Historic Preservation. A tour of this 1877 iron barque, built in Scotland, provides an exciting look at Galveston's seafaring past.

The ship and adjacent museum, with its superb permanent and visiting exhibits, are at Pier 21, at the foot of 22nd Street (409-763-1877). Open daily 10 a.m. to 5 p.m. Three blocks from the Strand, the **Grand 1894 Opera House,** 2020 Postoffice St. (800-821-1894; www.thegrand.com), is a distinctive, lavishly decorated theater whose stage has been graced with dignitaries from Anna Pavlova and John Philip Sousa to Hal Holbrook and Ray Charles. Restored to the tune of $7 million, the Grand offers a full schedule of renowned entertainment and popular musicals.

The downtown area is also a shopper's paradise. Look into the newly revitalized Gallery Row on Postoffice Street, just 3 blocks away. Among finds are Mod Coffee House, DesignWorks, and The Emporium at Eibands (read more at www.galveston.com /artgalleries).

Of course, there's always the beach to consider—and there's not been a better time to hang out on the sands of Galveston in several years. The most recent renourishment project placed over 500,000 cubic yards of sand for the cost of $10 million. The Texas General Land Office began Texas's largest project for the West End of the Island in mid-2010. Along Galveston's 4-mile-long Seawall, between 10th and 61st Streets, concessionaires rent lounge chairs and umbrellas on the sand, and there are rentals for bicycles and pedal-powered surreys to ride on the Seawall. That's where you'll also see the *See-Wall* **mural,** a 10-mile-long oceanic painting done by 14,000 members of the community. Galveston is also blessed with a pair of beach parks, **Stewart Beach at Second and Seawall** (409-765-5023), and **East Beach,** also called R. A. Apffel Park (Seawall at Boddeker; 409-762-3278). Alcohol-free Stewart is more family-oriented, with volleyball and food service. East Beach allows alcohol and on-the-beach parking, as well as sandcastle contests and live music.

Another option is **Galveston Island State Park,** 10 miles west from the Seawall via FR 3005 (409-737-1222). This is the spot for camping, bird-watching, nature hikes, and fishing on 1,950 acres of Gulf and bay lands on the island's western end.

DINNER **Saltwater Grill,** 2017 Postoffice St.; (409) 762-3474. Hands down, this is the favorite restaurant on the island. Fresh Gulf fish includes red snapper and oysters, but sensational fresh Chilean sea bass is featured in Shanghai Delight, with spinach, bok choy, and ginger-soy broth. Fresh mussels come from Maine, and clams are flown in from the Florida Keys.

LODGING **Tremont House,** 2300 Ship's Mechanic Row; (800) 996-3426 or (409) 763-0300. This romantic and sophisticated 1873 hotel has 117 lavishly appointed rooms. Guests have membership privileges at Galveston Country Club's eighteen-hole golf course, as well as the Hotel Galvez spa and pool a few blocks away.

DAY 3/MORNING

BREAKFAST **La Estacion,** (2428 Ball St.; 409-762-4262), serves up the best breakfast burritos bursting with eggs, bacon, and potatoes in homemade tortillas.

You have tough choices to make, as there are several good options for whiling away the day before your flight home.

First, you can spend the morning and early afternoon at **Moody Gardens Discovery Museum and IMAX Ridefilm Theater,** 1 Hope Blvd.; (800) 582-4673. At this 156-acre complex, there's a ten-story glass pyramid housing a lush rain forest, complete with appropriate birds, butterflies, bats, and fish; an amazing aquarium; and a large beach for swimming and sunning. The IMAX theater features a 180-degree wraparound screen showing such wild 3-D films as *African Adventure 3D: Safari in the Okavango; Ultimate Wave Tahiti 3D,* and *Wild Ocean 3D.* Open daily at 10 a.m. Check www.moody gardens.org for current listing of films and exhibits. The Discovery Museum features new exhibits every six months or so.

Kemah Boardwalk (281-488-7676; www.kemahboardwalk.com) is a booming multifaceted development in Galveston Bay that offers diversions in the way of amusement rides, wine bars, shops and galleries, and dining in a waterside setting with fountains and palm trees. Hit hard by Hurricane Ike, Kemah is back in business with fervor.

Or you can head back to Houston, where shopping is considered a full-time occupation. Go to the world-famous, original **Galleria** in Uptown Houston (5085 Westheimer Rd.; www.simon.com) to shop at Saks Fifth Avenue, Tiffany & Co., Ferragamo, Louis Vuitton, Lucky Brand Jeans, and much more. Near the **Galleria at Uptown Park** (8 Greenway Plaza; www.uptownparkhouston.com), find Ann Taylor Loft, Bill Walker Clothier, Hanson Galleries, the Cigar Vault, and Uptown Day Spa, among several exclusive retailers.

Just be sure to leave enough time to turn in your rental car and catch your flight home to the Dallas/Fort Worth area.

There's More . . . .

GALVESTON

The Lone Star Flight Museum, 2002 Terminal Dr.; (409) 740-7722; www.lsfm.org; now offers rides aboard such historic warplanes as the B-25, Steerman, B-17, and others.

Schlitterbahn Galveston Island (www.schlitterbahn.com/gal) has been voted the #1 Indoor water park in the U.S.

HOUSTON

Shopping: For premium denim lines, with late-night shopping and cocktails on the side, head to **310 Rosemont** in River Oaks (1965 W. Gray St.; no Web site). *Project Runway* fans are flocking to **Chloe Dao's Lot 8 Boutique** in Rice Village (6127 Kirby Dr.; www.lot8 online.com) for hot cocktail duds and trendy day togs.

Although it's been around since 1883, **Hamilton Shirts** is the place now run by young, fourth-generation owners that have turned the haberdashery into a more retail-friendly place (5700 Richmond Ave.; www.hamiltonshirts.com). Charlie Wilson is among famous clientele, who stop by (or visit online) to cherry-pick fabrics, cuffs, buttons, and cut on lovely custom shirts, $200 to $400 each.

If you're a sports fan, see what teams are in town. The Houston Astros play Major League Baseball downtown at **Minute Mail Park** and the NBA's Houston Rockets play a couple of blocks away at the **Toyota Center.** The Houston Texans play NFL teams at **Reliant Stadium,** and the world's largest rodeo, the **Houston Rodeo and Livestock Show,** takes places at Reliant, too, throughout Mar (www .visithoustontexas.com).

Other Recommended Restaurants & Lodgings . . . . .

GALVESTON

Mosquito Cafe, 628 14th St.; (409) 763-1010. A nice break from fried fish and Mexican food, this little spot near the University of Texas Medical Branch bowls you over with freshness with offerings such as pasta salad with spinach and chicken and sandwiches made with Jamaican jerk pork.

HOUSTON

Armando's, 2630 Westheimer Rd.; www.armandoshouston.com. The River Oaks landmark reminds us exactly what Mexico City elegance is, pampering palates with magnificent ceviche, sublime grilled snapper, signature queso flameado, and lethal margaritas.

Beaver's, 2310 Decatur St.; www.beavershouston.com. Star chef Monica Pope goes super-casual with an organic barbecue spot serving spicy ground lamb wraps incorporating almonds and dried fruit; fried pepperoncinis stuffed with cream cheese and pork; and smoked all-natural brisket.

Catalan, 5555 Washington Ave.; www.catalanfoodandwine.com. In the now-hot Washington Street corridor, chef Chris Shepherd knocks you out with his twist on tapas, such as crispy pork belly with pure cane syrup, foie gras bonbons with watermelon jelly, and cured salmon with lavender and honey.

Hilton Americas, 1600 Lamar St.; www.hilton.com. Big, contemporary and perfect for the convention crowd, this luxury hotel overlooks Discovery Green in downtown Houston.

Hotel Icon, 220 Main St.; www.hotelicon.com. Downtown's pretty boutique hotel in a 1911 former bank building puts you in easy reach of theaters and sports venues. Voice is the celebrated restaurant off the lobby.

Hotel ZaZa, 5701 Main St.; www.hotelzaza.com. The hotel opened in the Museum District to much acclaim in H-town's former Warwick building. Is it too hip for the neighborhood? Nah, ZaZa simply wows with posh rooms, concept suites (Rock Star, Casablanca—you get the drift), a fabulous spa, and pool cabanas.

Max's Wine Dive, 4720 Washington Ave.; www.maxswinedive.com. Grab a seat at the bar, drink a bottle of bubbly, nibble on supple bites of spicy alligator tail, buffalo sliders, and utterly perfect French fries while watching the nightlife in action.

KEMAH
Skipper's, 1026 FR 2094; (281) 334-4787. A bustling restaurant and bar with a good veggie omelet and piles of pancakes.

For More Information . . . .

Galveston Island Convention & Visitors Bureau; www.galveston .com.

Greater Houston Convention & Visitors Bureau; www.visithouston texas.com.

SOUTHBOUND ESCAPE *Two*

Port Aransas, Corpus Christi, and Kingsville (By Plane)

LAZY BEACH DAYS/2 NIGHTS

Mustang Island was a Texas barrier island frequented by romanticized pirate Jean Laffite and his buccaneer pals in the 1820s, so once in a while a grog-soaked treasure hunter searches for rumored buried pirate treasure. But what everyone finds on Mustang Island, once called Wild Horse Island, is riches in sand dollars and varied

> Beachcombing
> Seaside lodging
> Fresh fish
> Deep-sea fishing
> Aquariums
> Bird-watching
> Historic ranch

seashells just after high tide. The island's 18 miles of beach are cleaned daily, and the tar deposits we used to see have not been present for several years. Cars can drive on the beach as long as drivers purchase a $12 parking permit, which can be picked up at the chamber of commerce and at convenience stores.

The first phase of the new Port Aransas Nature Preserve gives you added options for taking in the great outdoors along the shore. Located just off the ferry landing along the Corpus Christi Ship Channel, the 1,217-acre preserve offers more than 2 miles of hike-and-bike trails within the park and includes a Pavilion, boardwalks over algal flats, crushed granite trails on the uplands, covered seating sites, and a tower overlooking wetland areas around Salt Island. Phase 2 will eventually add another 1.25 miles to the existing trail system and provide a link to the Leona Belle Turnbull Birding Center.

Near the ferry dock in Port Aransas, you will find several shrimp and fish shacks selling fresh seafood for rock-bottom prices. Stock

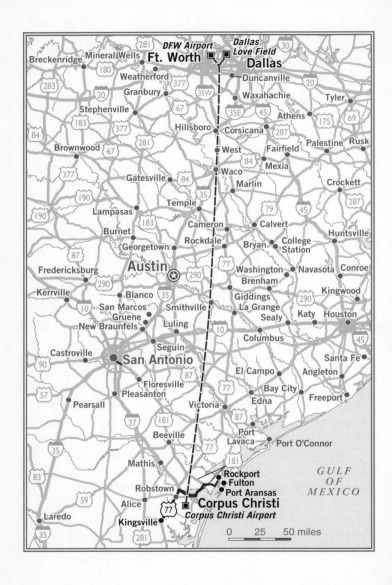

up on jumbo shrimp, and keep your vacation cheaper by cooking some meals in your rented condo's kitchen. Your days can be filled with long walks on the shore, horseback riding, Jet Skiing—or nothing at all.

DAY 1/MORNING

Driving to the beach from Dallas/Fort Worth defeats the Quick Escape purpose. All you have to do to make this an easy trip is board an early-morning plane to Corpus Christi from either DFW Airport or Love Field. Grab a pastry or breakfast sandwich at the airport. The flight is usually just under one hour. At the airport there, rent a car for your touring.

From **Corpus Christi Airport,** follow TX 358 East, following the signs to Port Aransas. Once in Port Aransas, get settled in your room or condo. If you're looking for one perfect beach, pack a picnic and drive about 14 miles south on TX 361 to **Mustang Island State Park** (361-749-5246). There are nearly 3,500 acres adorned with sand dunes, sea oats, and morning glory, and 5 miles of Gulf-front beach with camping, picnicking under arbors, a nature trail, a fish cleaning station, and showers. For a more private, open expanse of white sands, hop the **Jetty Boat** at Fisherman's Wharf (900 North Tarpon St.; 361-749-5448), for a fifteen-minute ride to San Jose Island. This uninhabited beach reserve is known for excellent shelling and picnicking; take fresh water and fishing gear, too.

Port Aransas has a trolley system to cart you around town for a 25-cent fare. The trolleys run continually each day from 10 a.m. to 5 p.m., with pickup points that include the Beach Access Road, the Birding Facility, the Marina, the Jetties, Horace Caldwell Pier, and the Mustang Beach Airport.

LUNCH   **Seafood and Spaghetti Works,** Alister at Avenue G; (361) 749-5666. Very popular, unique menu of seafood, steaks, Italian food, pizza, soup, and salad bar.

AFTERNOON

The **Port Aransas Birding Center,** operated by the city parks and recreation department (361-749-4158), teems with a variety of botanical planting and is a hub on the **Great Texas Birding Trail.** It's home to hundreds of permanent and visiting birds. Birders will enjoy spotting the buff-bellied hummingbird, seaside sparrow, white-tailed hawk, and crested caracara, as well as frigates, raptors, and all sorts of waterfowl. Find the center just off Ross, approximately 1½ miles from the ferry landing. Free, guided birding walks are offered at 9 a.m. on Wed.

Just for fun, have a look at the **Tarpon Inn,** 200 East Cotter Ave.; (361-749-5555). It was originally built in 1886 by a boat pilot and lighthouse keeper, who used surplus lumber from the nearby Civil War barracks. The inn burned, and its replacement was destroyed in the 1919 hurricane. The 1920s version still resembles old barracks. The Tarpon remains popular with anglers; boasts a list of notable guests, like Franklin D. Roosevelt; and is listed on the National Register of Historic Places. You don't want to miss seeing FDR's autograph on one of the 7,000 signed tarpon scales in the lobby.

DINNER   **Crazy Cajun,** 303 Beach St.; (361) 749-5069. This is the place for a Louisiana-style shrimp and crawfish boil: hot, fresh shrimp; crawfish; stone crab claws; new potatoes; corn on the cob; and smoked sausage. Gumbo and sourdough bread are good, too.

LODGING **Coral Cay Condominiums,** 1419 Eleventh St., Port Aransas; (361) 749-5111 or (800) 221-4981. Eighty-six condos front on the beach, with kitchens and cable TV.

DAY 2/MORNING

BREAKFAST In your condo. Otherwise, stop at one of the coffeehouses.

Better head out early to catch fish, since Port A, as the locals refer to it, calls itself the place "where they bite every day." Try for redfish, speckled trout, flounder, and drum in the surf at **South Jetty** and **Station Street Pier.** Group fishing aboard party boats such as the *Island Queen* gives anglers a chance to reel in bigger game fish. Rod, reel, and tackle are included for a flat price that changes from season to season. Private charters, which can cost in the hundreds, go in search of tarpon, sailfish, marlin, kingfish, mackerel, bonito, red snapper, amberjack, barracuda, yellowfin tuna, wahoo, and shark. Another fishing option is the more extensive excursion aboard the ninety-passenger *Scat Cat,* a catamaran making eleven- or twelve-hour trips into the Gulf. Reservations are accepted up to six months in advance, so book ahead (361-749-5448, 800-605-5448). For information on charter companies, ask at the **Port Aransas Chamber of Commerce** (see For More Information).

If you need still more time on the sand, drive southward on TX 361 about fifteen minutes to where Corpus Christi Bay meets Laguna Madre at the JFK Causeway, the roadway to **Padre Island National Seashore.** The legendary narrow island extends 113 miles down to Mexico and is the longest of all barrier islands on the Texas coast. No commercial development is allowed on this 80-mile, mid-island stretch, but National Park Service rangers provide information on camping and four-wheel-driving areas. Beachcombing and shell collecting are the national seashore's primary attractions, but federal law forbids taking flint points, coins, or anything that might be considered historical. Daily programs offered in summer by National Park Service rangers at **Malaquite Beach** include a 1 p.m. walk and study of the sea's natural flotsam and jetsam and a 2 p.m. in-water look at marine animals in Laguna Madre. Rangers also conduct fireside talks at dusk on Fri and Sat on a variety of island topics. Reach the National Park Service's Padre Island office on the mainland at (361) 949-8068, or call the Malaquite Beach ranger's office at (361) 949-8068.

LUNCH Two worthy and especially casual choices await. There's **Virginia's On the Bay** (815 Trout St.; 361-749-4088), an open-air spot on the water with a great view, plus good burgers and grilled fish; and **Trout Street Bar & Grill** (104 West Cotter Ave.; 361-749-7800), a cool waterside hangout serving shrimp remoulade, ceviche, crab cakes, Mediterranean shrimp scampi, grilled quail, and aged angus steaks.

AFTERNOON

Take the free car and passenger ferry to **Aransas Pass** (be aware that lines can be very long on weekends and holidays), and pick up TX 35 North for a few miles to the twin towns of **Rockport** and **Fulton.** Rockport, a seaside art colony, offers the **Rockport Center for the Arts** inside the restored 19th-century Bruhl-O'Connor home, at the point in **Rockport Harbor** (361-729-5519). Studios, classrooms, and four galleries are inside. Rockport Harbor is home, too, to the **Texas Maritime Museum,** 1202 Navigation Circle (866-729-2469, 361-729-1271), which showcases the state's seafaring heritage from early Spanish explorers and Texas's battle for independence to the development of dozens of deep-water commercial ports and offshore oil exploration. Exhibits include shipwreck relics approximately 450 years old, portraits of every ship that sailed in the **Texas Navy**, and a collection of watercolors of Texas lighthouses. Open 10 a.m. to 4 p.m. Tues through Sat and 1 to 4 p.m. on Sun.

Barely 5 miles north on TX 35 in Fulton, just past those eerily shaped, leaning cypress trees twisted by constant winds, is **Fulton Mansion State Historical Site,** 317 Fulton Beach Rd. at Henderson Street (361-729-0386). A four-story showpiece dating from 1876, this innovative home was uniquely outfitted at its beginning with central air-conditioning and hot and cold running water. A French Second Empire design graces the thirty-room mansion, restored by the state parks department. Visitors must wear soft-soled shoes to protect the floors. Open 10 a.m. to 3 p.m. Tues through Sat and 1 to 3 p.m. Sun.

Plan ahead to visit the **Aransas National Wildlife Refuge,** 37 miles north of Rockport via TX 35, between November and March, prime months for viewing the rare whooping cranes, which numbered only twenty-one in the 1940s. The United States and Canada made a sensational joint effort about fifty years ago to save these remarkable migratory birds, who journey annually from Canada in Oct and Nov to spend winter in these nesting grounds. The 55,000-acre asylum, now home to 140 whooping cranes, is operated by the U.S. Fish and Wildlife Service for the protection and management of almost 400 species of birds, including Canada geese, sandhill cranes, and pintail and baldpate ducks as well as white-tailed deer, javelina, and raccoons. View the birds from an observation point or aboard one of several boat tours that travel along the intracoastal canal from Rockport.

The refuge offers a 16-mile, paved tour road; an interpretive center/museum; several miles of walking trails; and a picnic area. Keep in mind that you'll need bug repellent; no food or gas provisions are on the grounds; and visitors should not feed any wildlife.

The refuge is open daily from sunrise to sunset. Contact the refuge's visitor center, FR 774 and FR 2040; (361) 286-3559.

One of the most popular whooping crane and dolphin tour outfits is **Rockport Adventures** (at Sandollar Pavilion in Rockport; 877-892-4737; www.rockportadventures.com), which offers close-up views of the endangered whooping cranes in the *M.V. Skimmer.* The trip covers 60 miles of wetlands and bays, including St. Joseph Island, Matagorda Island, Blackjack Peninsula, and, of course, the Aransas National Wildlife Refuge. The narrated tour (offered during the season, Nov–Mar) includes complete wildlife identification, complimentary binoculars, and a continental breakfast. Call for schedules and rates and information on dolphin tours and sunset cruises.

DINNER **Charlotte Plummer's Seafare Restaurant,** 202 North Fulton Beach Blvd., Rockport; (361) 729-1185. This is a longtime favorite for fans of fresh Gulf fish; appetizers include shrimp quesadilla and mango shrimp, entree choices range from crab cake po'boys and blackened fish sandwiches to whole flounder stuffed with crab, and pepper-crusted tuna—margarita and frozen daiquiri choices abound.

LODGING **Coral Cay Condos.**

DAY 3/MORNING

Cross over the Corpus Christi Ship Channel to the mainland. The drive is about forty-five minutes to Corpus.

BREAKFAST **Taqueria Acapulco,** 1133 Airline Rd., Corpus Christi (361-994-7274). Cheap Mexican eats, including authentic breakfasts, are served up here; specify mild or hot. Eggs migas is the best bet.

Visit the **Texas State Aquarium,** which opened in 1991 on Corpus Christi Beach at the Harbor Bridge (800-477-GULF or 361-881-1200). This expansive, impressive facility gets you up close and personal with animals and plants of the Gulf of Mexico, primarily via surrounding walkways that course through the exhibits by gigantic tanks filled with fish. Exhibits include a new dolphins showcase; along with Jellies: Floating Phantoms, which focuses on jellyfish; Otter Space, which offers a permanent home to Texas river otters; and Turtle Bend, a sanctuary for endangered Kemp's ridley sea turtles and green sea turtles. Open daily, with longer hours in summer.

Just a few blocks away, kids and adults both get a kick out of the **World of Discovery,** 1900 North Chaparral St. (361-883-2862). As the permanent dock for the Ships of Christopher Columbus, this is where today's discoverers can explore exact replicas of the *Niña, Pinta,* and *Santa Maria,* built by the government of Spain for the 500th anniversary of the great voyage. Next door, the **Corpus Christi Museum of Science and History**'s (www.ccmuseumdres.com) exhibits include the Smithsonian's Seeds of Change, which commemorates the impact of Christopher Columbus's voyages, as well as science and natural history displays that focus on energy, birds, gems and minerals, and shells. The hands-on children's area has a shrimp boat, bird costumes, and video phones, while Reptiles of South Texas features a live alligator, and "Shipwreck!" is the award-winning exhibit of the 1554 Spanish shipwreck off Padre Island. Lots of fun, especially on the rare rainy day.

LUNCH **Desiree's by the Bay,** inside the Corpus Christi Art Center, 100 Shoreline; (361) 887-7403. Try curried chicken salad, fish tacos, or a Reuben sandwich.

AFTERNOON

If time permits, consider a wonderful side trip (less than an hour's drive) from Port Aransas and Corpus Christi to Kingsville, southwest via TX 44 and US 77. Here you'll find the world-renowned **King Ranch,** founded in 1853 by Capt. Richard King. Today the King Ranch sprawls across 825,000 scrubby coastal plains acres that include black farmland, coastal marshes, and mesquite-infested pastures. At 1,300 square miles, the ranch could swallow the state of Rhode Island. King's descendants are active in the ranch's continuing workings, which include magnificent horse and cattle breeding.

Visits to the ranch tell the story of the birth of America's ranching industry. A National Historic Landmark, the ranch offers two familiarization videos at the visitor center and an introduction to the guided tours. You'll see some of the King family's historic buildings, or you can arrange for special-interest tours, such as bird watching. Some tours include stops at the famous **King Ranch Saddle Shop.** Find the King Ranch Visitor Center at Highway 141 West (361-592-8055 or 361-592-4040; www.king-ranch.com).

Another must-see is the **King Ranch Museum,** 405 North 6th St.; (361) 595-1881. Permanent collections include Toni Frissell's award-winning photographic essay on life at King Ranch in the early 1940s; saddles from around the world; guns, such as the King Ranch commemorative Colt Python .357 magnum revolver (serial number KR1); a limited-edition series of full-scale replicas of historic Texas flags; and antique carriages and vintage cars, including El Kineño, a custom-designed Buick Eight hunting car built for congressman R. M. Kleberg Sr. in 1949.

On the campus at Texas A&M/Kingsville, see the **John E. Conner Museum and the South Texas Archives** (361-595-2810). Among the permanent exhibits is the Caesar Kleberg Hall of

Natural History, which examines the ecosystems of the south Texas and northern Mexico biospheres. Slide shows and an award-winning video detail the wonders of a land where it seems as though "everything bites, stings, or can hurt you." The ranching area features a chuck wagon, branding irons, saddles, barbed wire, and small ranching equipment, while the Graves Peeler Hall of Horns displays 264 trophy mounts of North American game, including elk, moose, antelope, bighorn sheep, mountain goats, grizzlies, and white-tailed deer.

Say farewell to the ocean and head back to the Corpus airport for your flight home.

There's More . . . .

More guided boat tours into **Aransas National Wildlife Refuge,** about $20 to $25 per person. For a list of skippers, contact the Rockport-Fulton Chamber of Commerce at (361) 729-6445 or (800) 242-0071; www.rockport-fulton.org.

Sailing lessons are found at the **Yachting Center of Corpus Christi** (at the marina on Cooper's Alley L-head, Corpus Christi; 361-881-8503), with services for the beginner, intermediate, and advanced sailor by captains licensed by the U.S. Coast Guard.

Newport Dunes Golf Club (265 Palm Island Dr., Port Aransas; 361-749-4653; www.newportdunesgolf.com) is a gorgeous Arnold Palmer course unfolding along the seashore, distinguished as the first Texas golf course sitting right next to the Gulf of Mexico. Newport Dunes measures more than 6,900 from the back tees and is a par 71 course that gives you plenty of challenges in the way of wind from the ocean, rolling fairways, and fast greens.

Special Events & Festivals . . . .

LATE FEBRUARY

Whooping Crane Festival, Port Aransas; (800) 45-COAST; www .whoopingcranefestival.org. The ten-day event offers local birding events and tours, including those on land and water. There's a dolphin encounter boat tour, too, as well as photography field trips.

EARLY JULY

Deep-Sea Roundup, Port Aransas; (361) 749-5919. Oldest fishing tournament on the Texas coast, beginning with the Tarpon Rodeo in 1932.

Other Recommended Restaurants & Lodgings . . . . .

CORPUS CHRISTI

Beach Place Condominiums, 202 Reef Ave., No. 402; (361) 881-5100 or (800) 881-5110. Situated on Corpus Christi Beach, there are thirty-nine condos with one or two bedrooms, cable TV, private laundry room, and heated pool.

KINGSVILLE

B Bar B Ranch Inn, Farm Road 2215, 8 miles south of town via US 77; (361) 296-3331; www.b-bar-b.com. This charming B&B sits on an eighty-acre working ranch and offers six bedrooms in the ranch house and a separate pool house. Hunting trips for quail, deer, dove, and turkey are offered in appropriate seasons. Ask about special dinner menus on Fri and Sat evening.

PORT ARANSAS

Castaways Seafood & Grill, Alister at Beach; (361) 749-5394. Seafood, steaks, burgers, and chicken are presented in a nautical, historical setting.

For fully-equipped rental houses on Mustang Island, call **Coast-line Adventures Rental Management** (361-749-7635 or 800-656-5692) or Gulf Breeze Resort Management (361-749-3561 or 888-951-6381).

Dunes Condominiums, 1000 Lantana; (361) 749-5155 or (800) 288-DUNE. Eighty-six units with condos on the beach, a health club, tennis courts, a fish house, and swimming pool.

Port Royal Ocean Resorts, 6317 Texas 361; (800) 242-1034; www .port-royal.com. A beachside setting with 210 condos, a private beach boardwalk, and tennis courts, this one claims to have the state's largest swimming pool.

Rock Cottages, 603 East Ave. G; (361) 749-6360. One block from the beach, these twenty-seven cottages have kitchens and telephones, and pets are welcome.

Roosevelt's Fine Dining, 200 A East Cotter St., on the grounds of the historic Tarpon Inn; (361) 749-1540. Fine steaks, fresh seafood, and decadent desserts. Open for dinner, Wed through Sat and for Sunday brunch.

Shells Pasta & Seafood, 52 East Ave. G, Port Aransas; (361) 749-7621. Open for lunch and dinner, this is a place liked for its many blackboard specials, in addition to sautéed crab cakes and fresh catches. Closed on Tues.

ROCKPORT

Laguna Reef, 1021 Water St.; (361) 729-1742 or (800) 248-1057; www.lagunareef.com. Seventy rooms, a fishing pier and pool; continental breakfast.

Latitude 2802, 105 North Austin St.; (361) 727-9009; www.latitude2802.com. Adjacent to an art gallery, this fine-dining venue offers oysters on the half-shell, ceviche, escargot, fresh catches, duck, and steak. Open for dinner; closed Mon.

For More Information . . . .

Corpus Christi Convention and Visitors Bureau, 1823 North Chaparral St., Corpus Christi, TX 78401; (800) 766-2322; www.corpuschristicvb.com.

Kingsville Convention & Visitors Bureau, 1501 US 77 North, Kingsville, TX 78363; (800) 333-5032; www.kingsvilletexas.com.

Port Aransas Chamber of Commerce, 403 West Cotter St., P.O. Box 356, Port Aransas, TX 78373; (800) 452-6278; www.portaransas.org.

Rockport-Fulton Area Chamber of Commerce, 404 Broadway, Rockport, TX 78382; (800) 242-0071; www.rockport-fulton.org.

SOUTHBOUND ESCAPE *Three*
Brenham, Round Top, and Chappell Hill
(By Car or Plane)

THE BIRTHPLACE OF TEXAS/2 NIGHTS

Washington County in southeast Texas lies in rolling fields of spring wildflowers midway between Austin and Houston. Called the Birthplace of the Republic of Texas, its center is Brenham, but there is a handful of charming towns nearby. In season, visitors are generously greeted with sensational views colored by bluebonnets, pink and yellow Indian blankets, and pale pink primrose.

> Gentle countryside
> Republic of Texas roots
> Antiques
> Gardens
> Miniature horses
> Ranches
> Ice cream
> German settlement

DAY 1/MORNING

Drive south on I-35E (from Dallas) or I-35W (from Fort Worth) through the town of West (an hour's drive) to Waco, then head southeast on TX 6 through Marlin (two hours from home), Calvert, Bryan-College Station, and Navasota. Then turn south on TX 105 to the area bordered by Washington, Independence, Brenham, Chappell Hill, and Burton.

Or you can fly from DFW or Dallas Love Field airports to either Austin-Bergstrom International Airport (a thirty-minute flight) or Houston's William P. Hobby Airport (just under an hour flight), then drive about ninety minutes to Brenham.

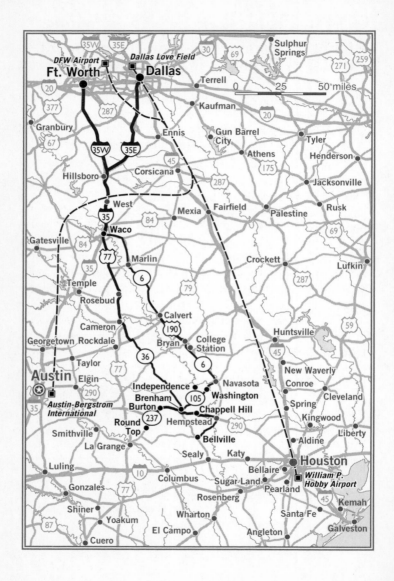

BREAKFAST   If driving, make plans to pause at **Czech Stop,** I-35, exit 353, West; (254) 826-4161. OK, yes, it's a gas station and convenience store—but it's so much more. There's a really good reason this place is packed day and night, and it has to do with the terrific on-site bakery. Here's where you can stock up on those Czech pastries called *kolaches,* filled with either sausage and cheese or with yummy fruit fillings, from blueberry and apricot to cherry and apple. Great sandwiches—try pastrami with Swiss or roast beef and cheddar—fill the deli cases.

Eat heartily, then head south to Waco and TX 6. Follow TX 6 to Navasota, where you'll take TX 105 through extraordinary rolling hills southwest to Washington-on-the-Brazos, legendary site of the 1836 signing of Texas's Declaration of Independence. From 1842 until 1846 Washington was also the capital of the republic and a commercial center for the prosperous Brazos Valley cotton trade. All is told at **Star of the Republic Museum,** at Washington-on-the-Brazos State Park, FR 1155 (936-878-2461; www.starmuseum .org). The exhibits of the star-shaped museum explain the history of Texas as a separate and exclusive nation and its journey to statehood. Open daily at 10 a.m. Seasonal exhibitions, audiovisual presentations, and demonstrations of early-19th-century life are often scheduled. In the park—renovated at a cost of $6 million—are part of a historic town site and the reconstructed Independence Hall; the home of Anson Jones, Texas's last president; and an outdoor amphitheater and lovely picnic grounds in an old pecan grove.

LUNCH   Head down FR 1155 to **Bevers Kitchen,** at 5162 Main St. in Chappell Hill; (979) 836-4178; www.bevers-kitchen.com. Try the meatloaf or fried chicken, but be sure to leave room for one of the renowned pies.

AFTERNOON

....

Wander west a few miles—through incredible wildflower vistas in spring—to the burg of Independence, another Washington County settlement, founded in 1824 by one of Texas's founding father Stephen F. Austin's original 300 families. **Old Baylor Park,** half a mile west on flower-peppered FR 390, home to the early Baptist college, Old Baylor University, contains ruins and the restored home of John P. Coles, a founding settler. Also on FR 390, the **Sam Houston Home** site is noted by a granite marker; a few yards away is **Mrs. Sam Houston's Home,** an early Greek Revival home the widow Houston bought for herself and her eight children after Sam died in 1863. Sam Houston Jr., other Texas pioneers, and veterans of wars from the American Revolution to World War II are buried in the town cemetery.

Now to Brenham, about 10 miles south of Independence via FR 50.

DINNER   **Country Inn Steakhouse,** 1000 East Blue Bell Rd., Brenham; (979) 836-2396. A place for beef, this favorite is known for its T-bone, ribeye, and chicken-fried steaks, as well as fish, shrimp, and burgers.

LODGING   **Ant Street Inn,** 107 West Commerce St.; (800) 481-1951 or (979) 836-7393. This restored, century-old hotel, just 1 block south of the courthouse square, offers rocking chairs on the balcony overlooking the courtyard, a bar, and fourteen guest rooms furnished in 19th-century antiques. Each room has a private bathroom, telephone and dataport, and cable TV. Hot breakfast is included. Visit the inn's website at www.antstreetinn.com.

For a country retreat, consider a hideout known as **Texas Ranch Life,** found about twenty minutes south of Brenham on the **Lonesome Pine Ranch** (866-839-2775 or 979-865-3649; www

.texasranchlife.com). Scattered across 1,600 rolling acres covered with native pecan trees and roamed by herds of longhorn cattle and buffalo are six historic homes—all expertly restored—and two modern dwellings. Whether you're a couple needing a romantic escape or a group of girlfriends or a family wanting lots of space to hang together, there's a house to suit you. While on the ranch, you can fish on any of eleven lakes, take riding lessons and head out on trail rides, participate in cattle roundups, enjoy hayrides and chuckwagon meals, hunt dove or quail, go bird watching, or simply go on long, peaceful walks. Breakfast is included, whether you want to eat with a group or have quiet mornings in your house.

DAY 2/MORNING

BREAKFAST At your bed-and-breakfast.

Spend time in the old-fashioned environs that characterize Brenham. Antiques shops are clustered downtown and around the square as well as on US 290, which leads east from town.

Another exploration of the past is found at the **Brenham Heritage Museum,** 105 South Market (979-830-8445; www.brenham heritagemuseum.org). Housed inside the 1915 U.S. Post Office, the museum—which moved in 1991—offers a permanent collection, including the Silsby steam fire engine, purchased by the city of Brenham in 1879 for $3,000. Open Wed from 1 to 4 p.m. and Thurs through Sat from 10 a.m. to 4 p.m.

Don't miss **Blue Bell Creameries,** just 2 miles southeast on Loop Farm Road 577 at 1101 South Blue Bell Rd., Brenham (979-836-7977 or 800-327-8135; www.bluebell.com). *Time* magazine called Blue Bell's the best ice cream in the world. This small-town giant now produces some twenty million gallons per year. Tours and samples are given to visitors on weekdays only. Visitors are also treated to a film and a look at production from an observation deck. The Blue Bell Country Store, which specializes in Blue Bell logo items and country-style gifts, is open Mon through Fri (and on Sat from Mar to Dec).

Eight miles north of town on FR 50 is **Antique Rose Emporium,** 9300 Lueckemeyer Rd. (979-836-5548). Once strictly a wholesaler of antique rose varieties, this is now a beautiful nursery open to the public. Antique roses, Texas natives, perennials, and herbs frame a restored 1855 stone kitchen, 1840 log corn crib, an early Texas saltbox house, and a Victorian home. Buy rosebushes on-site, or pick up a hefty catalog for mail orders.

In the same vicinity is the **Monastery of Saint Clare,** 9 miles northeast of Brenham on TX 105 (979-836-9652; www.monastery miniaturehorses.com). Cloistered nuns of the Order of Saint Clare, founded in the 13th century by a follower of Saint Francis of Assisi, breed, train, and sell gentle miniature horses on a ninety-eight-acre ranch. The tiny horses are scaled-down duplicates of their full-size cousins—Appaloosas, pintos, and Arabians—and are playful and endearing. This top breeding ranch unfolds along fertile slopes shaded by ancient, spreading oaks. There is a gift shop and a ceramics studio, too. Visitors are welcome between 2 and 4 p.m. Tues through Sat.

Head west on US 290 and south on TX 237—about 20 miles total—from Brenham to Round Top, population eighty-one. A little wide spot in the Fayette County road, Round Top took its name from Round Top Academy, which operated here from 1854 to 1867, when tuition cost $10 per semester. For information contact the **Round Top Chamber of Commerce** (979-249-4042 or 888-368-4783; www.roundtop.org).

LUNCH You have two choices on the Round Top square, both worth consideration: **Scotty & Friends,** 109 Bauer Rummel Rd. (979-249-5512), specialties include steaks, burgers, salads, and fried green tomatoes. They also serve breakfast Thurs through Sun. The other is **Royer's Round Top Cafe** (979-249-3611), a charming if tiny spot that serves inventive pasta dishes and grilled salmon and quail, as well as homemade pies. Open for lunch and dinner Wed through Sat and for lunch on Sun.

AFTERNOON

Bordering the east side of **Henkel Square,** in Round Top, is an impressive, growing collection of restored homes and buildings dating from 1820 until 1870. The furnishings and artistic decor are examples of the period's Anglo and German influences. The collection is administered by the Texas Pioneer Arts Foundation (979-249-3308; www.texaspioneerarts.org). Five blocks north, on TX 237, Festival Hill is home to the **International Festival Institute** (979-249-3129; www.festivalhill.org), whose monthly concert weekends and summer events feature visiting orchestras and string quartets; Festival Hill also has a fine array of magnificent, restored period buildings.

Go another 4 miles northeast of Round Top to the **Winedale Historical Center** at 3738 FM 2714 (979-278-3530; www.cah.utexas .edu/museums). Perfectly restored farms, ranch houses, plantation homes, log cabins, smokehouses, and barns represent more of the Anglo and German heritage prevalent in Texas. An extension of the University of Texas, it's open for weekday tours by appointment and at 9 a.m. Sat, noon on Sun. Winedale's many events throughout the year include a summer Shakespeare Festival, Oktoberfest, Christmas open house, and spring craft exhibition.

When you are ready to see another charming, historic town, make your way to Burton, about 10 miles west of Brenham on US 290 and 10 miles north of Round Top.

In this town of 311 residents, find the **Burton Cotton Gin,** 307 North Main St., (979-289-3378; www.cottonginmuseum.org), built in 1914. Now powered by a 1925 Bessemer twin-type IV oil engine, the working cotton gin is a restoration effort made possible by the guidance of the Smithsonian Institution and the National Trust for Historic Preservation. The project is meant to be part of a national museum complex for cotton ginning and cotton fiber production. Listed as a Texas Historic Landmark, on the National Register of Historic Places, and as a National Historic Mechanical Engineering Landmark, the gin offers guided tours.

DINNER   **Brazos Belle,** 600 Main St., Burton; (979) 289-2677; www.brazosbellerestaurant.com. Open for dinner only on Fri and Sat and lunch on Sun, this delightfully restored 1870s general store is loved for country French fare such as grilled salmon, beef medallions, and duck cassoulet.

An alternative is the **Burton Cafe,** on Washington in downtown Burton (979-289-3849; www.burtontexas.org/burtoncafe). A perfect country cafe, it serves changing daily specials, homemade breads, and fresh pies.

LODGING   Stay again in Brenham, or stay in Burton at **Knittel Homestead** (979-289-5102; www.knittelhomestead.com). An 1880-era Queen Anne Victorian home with wraparound porches, this inn is listed on the National Register of Historic Places and offers three bedrooms with private bath. A full country breakfast, beverages, and homemade cookies are included with stay.

DAY 3/MORNING

BREAKFAST   At your bed-and-breakfast.

Spend the morning exploring **Chappell Hill,** 10 miles east of Brenham via US 290. Listed on the National Register of Historic Places, Chappell Hill was established in 1847 and is filled with antebellum structures, antiques stores, a cigar-and-coffee shop, and vintage buildings. Stop in the **Chappell Hill Historic Museum** at 9220 Poplar St. (Chappell Hill Historical Society; 979-836-6033; www .chappellhillmuseum.org); it's open Wed through Fri 10 a.m. to 4 p.m. and Sun 1 to 4 p.m.

Also call for an appointment to tour **Stagecoach Inn** (979-830-8861; www.thestagecoachinn.com). Designated the most historic building in Chappell Hill, the gracious, two-story Greek Revival structure was built in 1850 by Mary Hargrove and her husband, Jacob Haller, just three years after they founded the town. Accommodations are available here, too.

Head toward home next, taking TX 36 North from Brenham to Cameron, where you'll take US 77 North to Waco. Or catch your plane back home from Austin or Houston. If driving, stop for lunch in Waco. After lunch, head north on I-35 to Dallas/Fort Worth.

LUNCH **Health Camp,** 2601 Circle Rd., just off I-35, Waco; (254) 752-2081. This legendary greasy-burger joint serves the most unhealthy but delicious chili dogs, tater tots, malts, and shakes in lots of flavors.

There's More . . . .

Blinn College, driving tour, 902 College Ave., Brenham; (979) 830-4152. Established in 1883, the college offers a blend of old and new architecture.

Historic homes tours, offered by the Independence Historical Society, Independence; (979) 830-5576; www.independencetx.com.

Two of Washington County's earliest homes and a rural one-room schoolhouse are shown.

Nueces Canyon Equestrian Center, 9501 US 290 West, 8 miles west of Brenham; (979) 289-5600 or (800) 925-5058; www .nuecescanyon.com. See world-class cutting horses in action and longhorn cattle, or go on a hayride and enjoy a barbecue buffet. There's a western gift shop, too, as well as a restaurant and lodging.

Pleasant Hill Winery, 1441 Salem Rd., Brenham; (979) 830-VINE; www.pleasanthillwinery.com. A countryside vineyard and winery offers free tours that begin and end in a reconstructed hilltop barn with a sensational view of the vineyard below. There's a great corkscrew collection and other winery artifacts, as well as wine sampling. The gift shop has wines and souvenirs for sale.

Rooster's Antiques, 6507 US 290 East, Brenham; (979) 830-5424; www.roostersantiques.com. Furniture and collectibles, plus coffee, pie, and ice cream.

Special Events & Festivals . . . .

LATE FEBRUARY THROUGH MARCH
Texas Independence Day Celebration, Washington-on-the-Brazos; (936) 878-2214; www.birthplaceoftexas.com. Costumed living history actors tell the story of Texas' signing of its declaration of independence from Mexico. Programs include activities for children and tours of historic buildings.

APRIL
Cotton Gin Festival, Burton; (979) 289-3378; www.cottongin museum.org. Arts and crafts fair with music and food.

MAY
Maifest, Brenham; (800) BRENHAM or (979) 830-5393; www .maifest.org. The weekend-long German festival is among the oldest of its kind in the South, with a history of more than 120 years. Parades, coronations, a children's carnival and music figure among a number of happenings during the festivities at Fireman's Park.

MID-SEPTEMBER
Washington County Fair; (979) 836-4112; www.washingtoncofair .com. With a claim of Texas's oldest county fair, this one offers Nashville entertainment, rodeos, carnival, country crafts, food and drinks, livestock and poultry, livestock auctions, and commercial exhibits.

MID-OCTOBER
Scarecrow Festival, Chappell Hill; (979) 836-6033; www.chappell hillmuseum.org/festivals.htm. More than one hundred arts and crafts booths, hayride tours of historic Chappell Hill, live entertainment, a food court, and artisans crafting old-fashioned wares.

NOVEMBER
Round Top Arts Festival at Henkel Square; (979) 249-3308. Juried art show, music, great food, pioneer arts demonstrations, and children's games.

EARLY DECEMBER

'Twas a Nineteenth-Century Christmas, Washington-on-the-Brazos State Historical Park; (936) 878-2214. Typical period activities, such as storytelling by candlelight, sing-alongs, toy making, and games for all ages.

MID-DECEMBER

Country Christmas in Chappell Hill; (979) 337-9910; www.chappellhillmuseum.org/hometour.htm. Festivities include a children's teddy bear parade, food and drink, shopping for Christmas goodies, and a visit from Santa.

Other Recommended Restaurants & Lodgings . . . . .

BELLVILLE

Silver Saddle Smokehouse, 312 East Main St.; (979) 865-8800; www.silversaddlebbq.com. Opened in spring 2010 by the owners of Texas Ranch Life, this barbecue joint features all-natural beef the Elicks raise on their ranch. There's also great smoked chicken and longhorn sausage. You can't help but admire the silver-festooned "Pancho Villa" saddle for which the restaurant is named.

BRENHAM

The Bread Basket Café, 210 East Alamo St.; (979) 421-9765. In the historic downtown. Offerings include breakfast all day, plate lunches starting at 10 a.m., homemade soups, stews, chili, salads, and sandwiches.

Far View Bed & Breakfast, 1804 South Park St.; (979) 836-1672 or (888) FAR-VIEW; www.farviewbedandbreakfast.com. Occupying a 2-city-block expanse, this 1925 Prairie-style home offers six guest rooms, five with private baths. A lavish breakfast is served in a formal dining room.

Nueces Canyon Ranch, US 290 West; (979) 289-5600 or (800) 925-5058; www.nuecescanyon.com. Stay in a private, three-bedroom, brookside guesthouse on this working, 135-acre horse ranch or in the ranch's twelve-room inn. Activities include horse-back riding, volleyball, and horseshoe pitching. For breakfast enjoy eggs, hash browns, sausage, kolaches, and fruit.

CHAPPELL HILL

Wakefield Farms Bed & Breakfast, 691 Pulawski School Lane; (979) 251-1459; www.wakefieldfarms.com. A 1855 German pri-vate cottage and 1843 private Greek Revival farmhouse each with bedrooms, bathrooms, and living areas. A country-style breakfast is served in a separate historic schoolhouse. Swimming pool and outdoor spa also on-site.

ROUND TOP

The Oaks Family Restaurant, 5507 TX 237, about 5 miles west of Round Top at Warrenton; (979) 249-5909; www.oaksfamilyrestau rant.com. Grab a table on the covered deck and dig in to a fabu-lous salad topped with shrimp, a jumbo burger platter, excellent chicken-fried steak or the Round Top Pizza, topped with olive oil, fresh basil, garlic, spinach, mushrooms, black olives, red onions, diced tomato, and feta cheese.

For More Information . . . .

Washington County Convention and Visitors Bureau, 314 South Austin St., Brenham, TX 77833; (979) 836-3695 or (800) BREN HAM; www.brenhamtexas.com.

SOUTHBOUND ESCAPE *Four*
Austin (By Car or Plane)
A CAPITAL RETREAT/2 NIGHTS

History
Art
Music
Quintessential Texas foods
Historic places
Architecture
Lakes
Bats

Austin embodies Texas's best qualities: It is vibrant and laid-back at the same time. As home base to state government and to one of the nation's largest universities, Austin is also strongly identified by its abundant live music. PBS's *Austin City Limits* originates here, of course, and SXSW (South by Southwest) is among the many major music festivals the city hosts.

The seat of Travis County, Austin has been a splendid place to just hang out for ages: Spaniards decided the Colorado River banks were perfect for a mission site in 1730, and that was after Native Americans had been established here for centuries. Originally called Waterloo, it became the capital under the new Republic of Texas president Mirabeau B. Lamar and was renamed for the "Father of Texas," Stephen F. Austin. With its rolling, tree-covered terrain; diverse cultural heritage; outstanding foods; and myriad entertainment choices, Austin is a top-notch escape.

DAY 1/MORNING

Take I-35E/W from Dallas/Fort Worth for the three-hour drive to Austin, or catch a thirty-five-minute flight from DFW Airport or from Dallas Love Field to Austin, then rent a car at the Austin airport. Pick up something for breakfast at the airport to take on your flight.

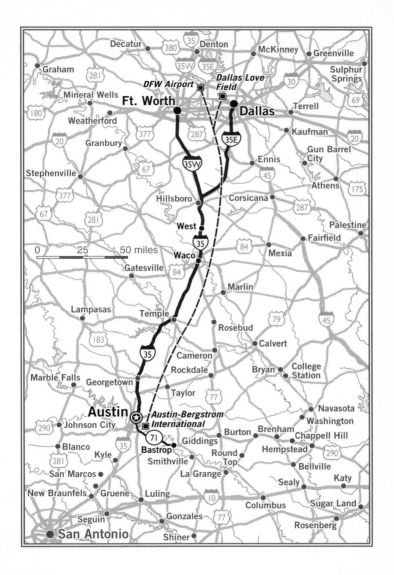

If driving, you'll see that after the two branches of the interstate meet in Hillsboro, you can exit at West for breakfast, a small Czechoslovakian community.

BREAKFAST Choose any of West's several *kolache* bakeries on Main and Oak Streets and on the access road along the interstate's east side. Most have little tables where you may sit and savor *kolaches* and coffee. Try the **Village Bakery,** 108 East Oak St. (254-826-5151), open since 1952. *Kolache* fruit choices are usually peach, apricot, blueberry, prune, and apple; heartier ones are klobasniki *kolaches* stuffed with Czech sausages.

A short drive south of West via I-35 is Waco. Pause in Waco, home to Baylor University and an old cotton-cattle commerce city that spreads across the historic Brazos River, on your way south. Originally claimed by the Hueco Indians, whose name the town bears, Waco hosted de Soto's men in 1542. Nearly 300 years later, the Texas Rangers established a fort here; the place was called Six-Shooter Junction during its Chisholm Trail days.

Have a walk along the historic **Suspension Bridge. Indian Spring Park** is on the west bank, and **Martin Luther King Jr. Park** is on the east bank. Within a few steps of the tourist center is the **Texas Ranger Hall of Fame and Museum,** Fort Fisher Park (254-750-8631). Exhibits include a replica of an 1837 Texas Ranger fort; dioramas; displays that detail the history of the Texas Rangers since Stephen F. Austin founded the Rangers, legendary law enforcement officials, in 1823; a firearms collection; Native American artifacts; and Western art. The Rangers are currently working on a new building that will serve as home to today's Company F, Texas Rangers. Picnic sites are available in the thirty-seven-acre park. Open daily 9 a.m. to 5 p.m.

And don't miss the **Dr Pepper Museum,** 300 South 5th St. (254-757-1025; www.drpeppermuseum.com). It's in the original

1906 bottling plant, which is on the National Register of Historic Places. Inside are a restored period soda fountain and much Dr Pepper memorabilia, plus audiovisual exhibits. This favorite Texas drink was originally mixed at Waco's Old Corner Drug Store in the 1880s. Open 10 a.m. to 5 p.m. Mon through Sat, noon to 5 p.m. on Sun.

From Waco continue 90 miles south on I-35 to Austin. Upon arriving in Austin, you'll see an important landmark on the horizon: the tower rising from the **University of Texas** (UT) campus (Martin Luther King Boulevard and 26th Street; 512-471-7703), which spreads over 357 acres between Guadalupe and I-35. Opened in 1882, the university has an enrollment of about 50,000 students. A good place to explore is **The LBJ Library and Museum,** 2313 Red River Rd. (512-721-0200; www.lbjlibrary.org). It is interesting even to nonfans of late president Lyndon Baines Johnson. Among the memorabilia on display are early family photos, a fourth-grade report card, a letter to his grandmother written during college expressing his deep desire to fit in, and engagement photos of LBJ and Claudia "Lady Bird" Taylor.

Another UT campus site is the **Harry Ransom Humanities Research Center,** 21st and Guadalupe Streets (512-471-8944; www.hrc.utexas.edu). There you'll find a rare, complete copy of the Gutenberg Bible and, from the photography collection, the world's first photograph, shot in 1826 by Joseph Niepce. New additions to the collections are Robert DeNiro's personal film collection including costumes, scripts, and photos. The literary collection includes Dylan Thomas and E. M. Forster first editions, and the Hoblitzelle theater arts collection contains Harry Houdini's personal correspondence and Burl Ives folk recordings. Open at 10 a.m. Mon through Sat, 1 p.m. Sun.

While at the Harry Ransom Center, have a look at the **Jack S. Blanton Museum of Art,** UT's fine arts museum (512-471-7324; www.blantonmuseum.org). The permanent collection is rich with some 13,000 works that span the history of Western civilization, from ancient to contemporary periods, including a significant collection of Latin American art and the 20th-century American art collection; a specific feature is a collection of American paintings, loaned by Mari and the late James Michener, who died in Austin in late 1997. The second phase of the museum houses educational facilities and offers a number of programs for the public. Among events is a monthly art party on the first Friday of the month, called "B Scene." The gallery is open daily.

LUNCH **Threadgill's,** 301 West Riverside Dr.; (512) 472-9304; www .threadgills.com. This Austin institution, originally located on North Lamar, was established in 1933 by Kenneth Threadgill, "the Grandfather of Austin Country Music." This newer site occupies the former music mecca called the Armadillo World Headquarters. The food is unbelievably good home-cooking, from baked chicken, chicken-fried steak, and meat loaf to platters of fresh, delicious vegetables and mammoth servings of pie, cake, and cobbler. The Texas neon-sign collection is amazing, too.

AFTERNOON
....

Continuing the cultural day, see the **French Legation Museum,** 802 San Marcos St. (512-472-8180; www.frenchlegationmuseum.org). This 1841 French Provincial cottage of Bastrop pine with French fittings was home for Comte Alphonse de Saligny, the French ambassador to the Republic of Texas. Operated by the Daughters of the Republic of Texas, the house-museum, situated behind grand iron gates atop a little hill, is furnished with 19th-century antiques and authentic French Creole kitchen items. Open from 1 to 5 p.m. Tues through Sat.

The **Elisabet Ney Museum,** 304 East 44th Street at Avenue H (512-458-2255; www.ci.austin.tx.us/elisabetney), is one of the country's four existing studios of 19th-century sculptors. It showcases the German immigrant sculptor Ney, a staunchly independent artist who came to the United States in 1873 and built this studio in 1892. Some Ney works are displayed here; others are at the Smithsonian National Museum of Art, in European palaces, and in the Texas statehouse. Opens at 10 a.m. Wed through Sat and at noon Sun.

Or opt to see the **O. Henry Museum,** 409 East 5th St. (512-472-1903). This quaint Victorian was occupied by the master of short stories and surprise endings. William Sydney Porter (his real name) briefly owned a publication called *Rolling Stone* from Austin in the 1890s. A yellowing original of *Rolling Stone* and various personal items are exhibited. Each spring the O. Henry Pun-Off provides a good time. Open at noon Wed through Sun.

At dusk, remember that it's time to watch the bats. Austin is home to the largest urban bat colony in North America. Some one and a half million Mexican free-tailed bats—now known as Austin's Official Animal—live beneath downtown's historic Congress Avenue Bridge, which spans Lady Bird Lake (part of the Colorado River). When night starts to fall from Apr through Oct, the bats fly out all at once, much to the pleasure of thousands of spectators who line the bridge and riverbanks.

DINNER **Iron Works Barbecue,** 100 Red River St.; (512) 478-4855. Touted by experts as one of Texas's finest barbecue establishments, this place provides excellent smoked pork ribs, pork loin, and beef brisket. Also wonderful and just down the street is **Stubb's,** 801 Red River St.; (512) 480-8341. A Lubbock-based monument to pecan-smoked meats, this joint has great chicken, brisket, and ribs—and live music.

Austin's evening music scene has been graced by notables including Stevie Ray Vaughan, Jerry Jeff Walker, Willie Nelson, the Fabulous Thunderbirds, Joe Ely, and many others from rock, country, jazz, blues, and Tejano arenas. While 6th Street was long known for its live music, it's now mostly filled with DJ clubs. You can find great live music in the **Warehouse District,** on the southern edge of downtown proper. Clubs like Antone's, Cedar Street, The Belmont, and others are dependable venues for the music scene; check the alt-weekly *Austin Chronicle* (www.austinchronicle.com) for schedules.

LODGING **The Inn at Pearl Street,** 809 West Martin Luther King Jr. Blvd.; (512) 478-0051 or (800) 494-2261. Surrounded by porches and a huge deck shaded by aged trees, this century-old Greek Revival estate is within walking distance of the university and downtown. Nine guest rooms, gorgeous common areas (including a music room and library), and nice touches like wine, large-screen TV, and in-room TV and VCR make this special. European breakfast on weekdays and a full breakfast on weekends.

If you want a place with golf and spa options, you must check into **Barton Creek & Spa,** 8212 Barton Club Dr.; (866) 572-7369; www.bartoncreek.com. In spring 2010, the Austin resort finished a widespread renovation of the spa, guest rooms, club house, and dining venues. A posh new women's boutique opened off the lobby, and a sizable patio pavilion extends the Hill Country Dining Room space. The ultimate guys' hangout is the Rock House, a renovated historic cottage on the golf course, with a cigar bar and billiards room. The updated fitness center overlooks wooded terrain, and the expanded spa facilities include a meditation room that opens onto a live, ancient cave trickling with spring water. Note that rates in summer can be especially affordable.

DAY 2/MORNING

BREAKFAST At your B&B. Or go for a Mexican breakfast to be revered at **Cisco's,** 1151 East 6th St. (512-478-2420). An Austin institution, this friendly Mexican bakery/cafe offers huevos rancheros, huevos migas (eggs with tortilla pieces and vegetables), and picadillos (homemade rolls stuffed with spicy beef).

Allow all morning to explore the **Capitol Complex,** starting with the dynamic **Bob Bullock Texas State History Museum,** Martin Luther King, Jr. Boulevard at North Congress Avenue (512-936-8746; www.thestoryoftexas.com). This unforgettable educational institution tells the story of Texas through a sensational variety of exhibits and interactive programs. A few steps away, tour the magnificently restored Capitol Visitor Center at 112 East Eleventh St. (512-305-8400; www.tspb.state.tx.us/CVC/home/home.html). Before entering the capitol building, you'll find a good introduction through historical exhibits, a gift shop, a Travel Information Desk, special exhibitions, and guided tours. The magnificent capitol was made of pink granite quarried in the Hill Country and is the tallest in the United States. Begun in 1882, the building was finished six years later.

LUNCH **Texas Chili Parlor,** 1409 Lavaca St.; (512) 472-2828. In a funky saloon setting, sample mean-as-hell chili for brave palates, or tacos, burgers, or salads. Or try another legendary dive, **Dirty's,** 2808 Guadalupe St.; (512) 477-3173; also called Martin's Kumbak, a burger stand since 1926 that serves onion rings, shakes, cold Shiner beer, and sandwiches.

AFTERNOON

A great natural resource of Texas is grandly displayed at the **Lady Bird Johnson Wildflower Center,** a 42-acre, $9.5 million site at 4800 Lacrosse Ave. (512-292-4200; www.wildflower.org). Lady Bird Johnson generously established this center in 1982 and remained a dedicated champion to the beautification of America with horticulture up until her passing in July 2007. The center is considered an authority on the conservation and reproduction of native plants and supports a nationwide educational program for various state highway departments' landscaping and beautification efforts. Visit to see various wildflowers, shrubs, trees, and plants or attend seminars, workshops, or classes. The gift shop sells seeds, calendars, note cards, T-shirts, and posters.

Cool off at the 400-acre **Zilker Park,** 2220 Barton Springs Rd. (512-476-9044), home to **Barton Springs Pool,** a 1,000-foot-long, rock-walled swimming pool that is always 69 degrees. Grassy, shady lawns slope to the pool; note that it's closed on Thurs. The park is also home to the Botanical Garden Center, the Austin Nature Center, a miniature train, and 8 miles of hiking and biking trails.

See the Hill Country's legendary sunset from northwest of town, following RR 2222 to RR 620. At the **Oasis,** RR 620 at Comanche Trail on Lake Travis (512-266-2442), crowds gather on seventeen wooden decks every afternoon to quaff cool drinks, munch on chips and salsa, and applaud the sun as it exits an orange-and-purple-splashed sky. The food here's not great and the drinks are expensive, but the setting is unbeatable.

DINNER **Hudson's on the Bend,** 3509 RR 620; (512) 266-1369; www .hudsonsonthebend.com. Pricey but worth every penny. The finely tuned entrees include pecan-grilled shrimp over creamy artichoke pasta, venison, elk, lamb chops in three sauces, and salmon-scallop terrine. Reservations a must; open nightly for dinner.

LODGING Another good idea is the **Driskill Hotel,** 604 Brazos St.; (512) 474-5911. Built in 1886, the magnificently renovated Driskill has a back door on 6th Street. There are 177 rooms; the best are in the original part of the building. Paintings and historical items, with period reproduction furniture.

DAY 3/MORNING

BREAKFAST At the **Driskill Hotel** or at **Kerbey Lane Cafe,** 3704 Kerbey Lane (512-451-1436) or 2700 South Lamar St. (512-445-4451). Healthily prepared goodies such as whole-wheat banana pancakes and black-bean breakfast tacos are offered.

If you'd like to do your body, mind, and soul a tremendous favor, book a day of massage, facial, body wrap, and reflexology at **Lake Austin Spa Resort** (1705 South Quinlan Park; 512-372-7300 or 800-847-5637)—or simply check in for one of this heavenly spot's three-, four-, or seven-day packages. In any case, you'll leave feeling better than you've ever felt, inside and out.

Originally a fishing camp when opened in the 1940s, this resort has through the years been a lakeside music and dancing hangout, a nudist camp, a rodeo-riders' camp, and then a "fat farm." Today, female and male guests come to get centered with days of yoga, stretching, water exercise, kickboxing, bicycling, hiking, and walking. Private, personal training and nutritional counseling are available, and a full menu of treatments is offered at the magnificent new spa complex.

The "stealth-health" food—all made with low-fat preparations—is outstanding: Meals typically include such choices as gingerbread pancakes with turkey bacon, lamb-and-vegetable skewers with couscous, and hot, sweet-and-sour snapper, but the menu changes weekly. You'll always find intriguing dishes. Special weeks of cooking and nutrition classes are offered.

Especially enticing are the resort's garden suites, with giant tubs that sit next to a garden courtyard and porch sitting areas that look out on gorgeous Lake Austin. In the quiet of the morning and evening, deer wander onto the grounds to feed and drink.

Make time, if possible, to take a side trip to another place in time. Following TX 71 East from south Austin about thirty miles, you'll wind up in **Bastrop.** Initially a meeting site for the Tonkawas and other Native Americans, the town was an important Colorado River crossing on the Camino Real. In 1821 Stephen F. Austin traveled through the area and decided to build a settlement, which was finally granted by the Mexican government in 1827. Three Bastropians were signers of the Texas Declaration of Independence, eleven died at the Alamo, and about sixty fought at the Battle of San Jacinto.

What's charming about Bastrop today is its historic downtown. **Maxine's Restaurant** at 905 Main St. (512-303-0919) has a menu of chef salad, chicken and dumplings, catfish, pork chops, burgers, and steak sandwiches.

Also worth a look are turn-of-the-20th-century buildings such as the Old Bastrop Jail and Courthouse, 802–804 Pine St.; the New England–style Bastrop Christian Church, 1104 Church St.; and the Bastrop Opera House, 711 Spring St. For bicycle rentals and information, stop in the **Bastrop Chamber of Commerce** office at 927 Main St. (512-321-2419).

Before making your way back to the Dallas/Fort Worth area, have an early dinner at the impressive new **Hyatt Regency Lost Pines Resort & Spa,** an elaborate resort with spa, golf, and horseback riding, about 9 miles west of Bastrop off Texas 71 (512-308-1234; www.lostpines.hyatt.com). Spread over 700 hilly, pecan-studded acres along the lovely Colorado River and next to the McKinney Roughs Nature Preserve, the resort will make you wish you were extending your trip by a few days. Meals at the **Firewheel Cafe** include cornmeal-crusted trout, Lost Pines Chili, and Texas Trail Brick-Oven Pizza.

Head home, driving north on I-35. Or catch a short flight home to DFW Airport or Dallas Love Field.

There's More . . . .

For shopping, look downtown in the **2nd Street District** (www.2ndstreetdistrict.com) for all kinds of cool high-end boutiques; and **Heritage Boot,** 117 West 8th St. (512-326-8577; www.heritageboot.com), for fancy, vintage-style boots designed by the owner himself.

The Long Center for the Performing Arts, 701 West Riverside Dr. (512-457-5100; www.thelongcenter.org), is a recent addition to town that hosts performances by the Austin Symphony, Austin Lyric Opera, and Ballet Austin. Also, its black box theater has shows by some super cool and edgy local groups like Salvage Vanguard and the Rude Mechanicals.

Good nightlife options now include **Justine's,** 4710 East 5th St. (512-385-2900; www.justines1937.com), with live music and French bistro fare; **East Side Show Room** 1100 East 6th St. (512-467-4280; www.eastsideshowroom.com), a live music destination with fabulous, "gourmet" cocktails; **The Good Knight,** 1300 East 6th St. (512-628-1250; www.thegoodknight.net), a spot for classic cocktails and upscale comfort food.

Funky dining abounds on South Congress, where the explosion of food trailers leads a national trend. At press time, more than 1,500 mobile restaurants were licensed in Austin, and most palates agree the best are on in SoCo. Try Lucky J's Chicken and Waffles, East Side King, and Hey Cupcake.

Special Events & Festivals . . . .

MARCH
South by Southwest Music Festival. See 1,800 bands in more than eighty music venues around town; (512) 467-7979.

APRIL
Wildflower Days Festival, Lady Bird Johnson Wildflower Center; (512) 292-4200. Among many attractions during the two-month spring celebration are gardening workshops and an especially

popular Art and Artisans Festival, showcasing work from more than 20 artists in media such as painting, metal, photography, pottery, and jewelry.

Other Recommended Restaurants & Lodgings . . . . .

AUSTIN

Carrington's Bluff, 1900 David St.; (512) 479-0638 or (800) 871-8909. On grounds spreading over an acre on a high bluff in the middle of town is an 1877 English-style country home that was part of an original homestead of the Republic of Texas. Rooms have private baths and are filled with antiques. There's a lovely porch, lawns, and gardens beneath a five-hundred-year-old oak. A full breakfast is included.

Fonda San Miguel, 2330 West North Loop; (512) 459-4121. Crowds here love the shrimp-scallop-crab cocktail, red snapper Veracruz, enchiladas in poblano mole, and steak in mild chile sauce.

Hotel Saint Cecilia, 112 Academy Dr.; (512) 852-2400; www .hotelsaintcecilia.com. Sister to the Hotel San Jose, this stylish new offering in the SoCo district takes its inspiration from creative spirits that include William Burroughs, the Rolling Stones, and Andy Warhol. Find five suites, six poolside bungalows, and three studios on wooded property.

Hotel San Jose, 1316 South Congress Ave.; (512) 444-7322. A dramatic renovation (and a hotelier with extreme vision) turned a rundown 1940s motor court into one of the nation's showplace boutique hotels. Contemporary, cool, and sexy, this little inn offers bungalow-style rooms in the super-hip SoCo neighborhood, full of great dining and music venues. There's a great music and video library, coffee shop, pool—and it's dog-friendly.

Jeffrey's, 1204 West Lynn St.; (512) 477-5584. Best bets are duck-mushroom soup, osso buco in smoked tomato-bourbon sauce, halibut with pine nuts and plum-rosemary sauce, and cranberry crème brûlée. Dinner only. Reservations recommended.

Kimber Modern, 110 The Circle; (512) 912-1046; www.kimber modern.com. Very chic and European, this new addition to South Congress (SoCo) district offers breakfast and happy hour daily.

Lambert's Downtown Barbecue, 401 West 2nd St.; (512) 494-1500. Found inside the historic Schneider Brothers Building in a refurbished old corner of downtown, this chic but very casual dining spot will knock you out with wood-smoked Wagyu beef ribs, prime rib, and coffee-rubbed brisket, as well as dry-aged rib eye steaks, Hawaiian ahi tuna, and desserts like Dr Pepper cake and fried blackberry pie. Live music most nights, too.

Uchi, 801 South Lamar Blvd; (512) 916-4808; www.uchiaustin .com. Super-hip Japanese restaurant from chef Tyson Cole brings the best sushi in Austin to your plate. It's always busy, so be prepared to wait for a table. Great wine selection, too. Open daily for dinner.

Vespaio, 1610 South Congress Ave.; (512) 441-6100. A dinner-only place, this favorite has garnered high praise for its carpaccio, chile-fired roasted chicken with polenta, and good wine list.

LOCKHART

Kreuz's Market, US 183; (512) 398-2361. A lunch side trip leads to Kreuz. Take US 290 across I-35 about 5 miles, turn south on US 183, and drive 30 miles to Lockhart. The restaurant stays busy all day; frequently the barbecue—which is cut to order—sells out by mid-afternoon. Get smoked brisket, pork chops, or sausage on a sheet of brown butcher paper, then go to the counter in the lunch room for sliced onion, tomato, cheese, avocados, jalapeños, pickles, and white bread. Don't look for barbecue sauce; if you can handle it, use the hot pepper sauce available in bottles on the tables.

For More Information . . . .

Austin Convention and Visitors Bureau, 209 East 6th St., Austin, TX 78701; (866) 462-8784; www.austintexas.org.

SOUTHBOUND ESCAPE *Five*

New Braunfels and Wimberley (By Car or Plane)

RIVERS AND EUROPEAN FLAVORS/2 NIGHTS

This escape offers plenty of the European heritage that flavors Central Texas. New Braunfels, seat of Comal County, has what should have been a most romantic history. Settled in 1845 by a German prince and his 200 followers, New Braunfels was named for the

- German heritage
- Antiques and collectibles
- River recreation
- History and architecture
- Family resorts

prince's hometown. In this New World spot he planned a castle for his fiancée, Princess Sophie, but she had no interest in his rough, unknown settlement. He returned to her and never saw Texas again.

Your wanderings will also lead you on a side trip to Wimberley, a resort town between two of the Hill Country's most pleasant streams, Cypress Creek and the Blanco River. A hub of shopping activity on weekends, when dozens of pottery studios, art galleries, antiques shops, and boutiques are open for business, Wimberley has a long list of very appealing bed-and-breakfast choices.

DAY 1/MORNING

Whereas this was once an easy jaunt down I-35, that's no longer the case. Congestion on the interstate has been relieved somewhat around Hillsboro, thanks to the widening of the expressway through that growing area, but traffic bogs down in maddening ways around Austin, although toll roads have helped lighten the load. But for this to be a quick trip, you really need to hop a plane for San Antonio.

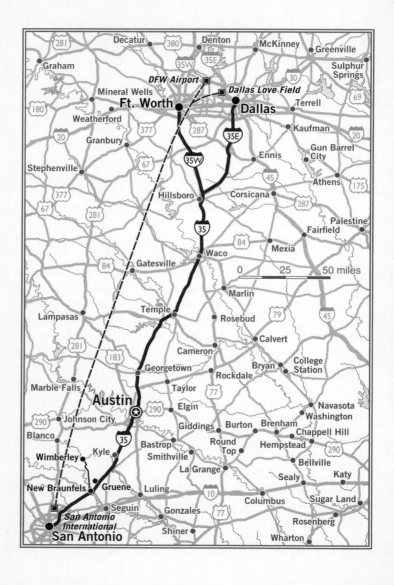

Take an early flight from DFW Airport or from Dallas Love Field, hop in your rental car, and make tracks from San Antonio westward into the legendary Texas Hill Country. Pick up breakfast at the airport to tide you over until lunchtime.

From San Antonio, it's just a twenty- to thirty-minute drive north on I-35 to New Braunfels. For a briefing on this pretty German burg, stop at the **Sophienburg Museum,** 401 West Coll St. (830-629-1572; www.sophienburg.org), named for the prince's bride even though she was a "no-show." The museum exhibits tell the story of German settlement through the region. A period bakery and pharmacy have been re-created. Opens at 10 a.m. Tues through Sat.

Also check out the **Museum of Texas Handmade Furniture,** 1370 Church Hill Dr. (830-629-6504; www.nbheritagevillage.org). The local German heritage society operates in this 1858 home.

DINNER **Huisache Grill,** 303 West San Antonio St. (830-620-9001; www.huisache.com), named for the small, scrubby tree found across the Hill Country, west Texas, and New Mexico, and pronounced "wee satch." The food is an excellent, creative mix of things like grilled shrimp salad, bratwurst and cheeses, sautéed wild mushrooms with Brie, grilled rosemary quail, and herb-crusted salmon. Nice beer and wine selection, too.

LODGING **Prince Solms Inn,** 295 East San Antonio St.; (830) 625-9169 or (800) 625-9169; www.princesolmsinn.com. A luxury bed-and-breakfast with fourteen rooms, this small inn is filled with antiques.

DAY 2/MORNING

BREAKFAST At the **Prince Solms,** or **Naegelin's Bakery,** 129 South Seguin Ave.; (830) 625-5722 or (877) 788-2895; www.naegelins.com. The oldest bakery in Texas, Naegelin's has been offering wonderful pastries, breads, and cakes since 1868.

Then it's time to get wet. **Schlitterbahn Waterpark,** 400 North Liberty Avenue in New Braunfels (830-625-2351; www.schlitterbahn .com/nb), has chutes, a surf ride, tons of tubing, seventeen waterslides, five kiddie parks, pools, hot tubs, an uphill roller coaster, water volleyball, and more. On New Braunfels's Comal River, Schlitterbahn has cottages and rooms, too. In the 310-acre **Landa Park**, Landa Street in New Braunfels (830-608-2163 or 830-608-2169), you can tube the Comal and then ride down a fun chute in adjacent **Prince Solms Park.** Landa Park also has glass-bottom boat rides, boat rentals, a miniature train, swimming in an Olympic-size pool or a natural spring-fed pool, miniature golf, and a standard golf course.

For Guadalupe River adventuring head to the north end of town and find the restored historic district called Gruene. Several river outfitters (call 830-629-5077 or check www.touringtexas.com/gru ene for a list) offer trips lasting anywhere from three to five hours. Midweek escapists may experience a lonely, peaceful trip of yore, but weekenders will join huge populations of high-spirited rafters and tubers who clog and trash the river. Rafting, canoeing, kayaking, and tubing are among the options; an early start is highly recommended.

One outstanding outfitter for river tripping is **Gruene River Company,** 1404 Gruene Rd. (830-625-2800; www.grueneriver company.com). Most of the guided and self-guided trips last about three hours. Like all outfitters, GRC will have you sign a standard release waiver. And remember, it's best to wear swimwear and tennis shoes while rafting and tubing (litterbugs sometimes leave beer bottles about), and sunblock is important, too.

LUNCH **Janie's Table,** in the Gruene Historic District; (830) 629-6121. A delightful, casual spot in a shady turn in Gruene Road, this place has unbeatable burgers, barbecue sandwiches and plates, frosty margaritas and longnecks, as well as homemade desserts such as Guadalupe mud cake and blackberry cobbler.

AFTERNOON

Spend a couple of hours exploring tiny **Gruene Historic District,** where shops sell antiques, clothing, housewares, wine, and leather goods. A few good ones to check out are **Gruene General Store** (830-629-6021; www.gruenegeneralstore.com), **Cactus Jack's Antiques** (830-620-9602), **Gruene Antique Company** (830-629-7781; www.grueneantiqueco.com), and **Texas Homegrown** (830-629-3176; http://texashomegrown.goods.officelive.com). Look around **Gruene Hall** (830-606-1281; www.gruenehall.com), Texas's oldest dance hall and a place to have a great time when a band is playing.

DINNER **Gristmill,** 1287 Gruene Rd.; (830) 625-0684; www.gristmill restaurant.com. A huge regional favorite, this restored cotton-gin mill has a spread of stone-and-wood dining areas and wonderful chicken-fried steak, fried catfish, steaks, burgers, and icy margaritas. There's live music on the patio in the evening. After dinner, check out the live music next door at Gruene Hall.

LODGING Prince Solms Inn.

NIGHTLIFE Evenings are never dull at **Gruene Hall.** Find rising stars in Texas music playing foot-stompin', two-steppin' favorites here every weekend. It's also known for rollicking Sunday Gospel Brunch gatherings, too.

DAY 3/MORNING

BREAKFAST **Prince Solms Inn,** or **New Braunfels Smokehouse,** Highways 81 and 46; (830) 625-2416; www.nbsmokehouse.com. Extensive breakfast buffet.

You'll need an early start, because this morning is filled with options. First, you can head west on Texas 46 about 17 miles to **Natural Bridge Caverns,** TX 46 at FR 1863 (210-651-6101; www

.naturalbridgecaverns.com). Named for the caverns' 60-foot, natural limestone bridge, this U.S. Natural Landmark offers gargantuan underground rooms—140 million years old and still growing—to explore. The corridors stretch for more than a mile, lead to Purgatory Creek, and are naturally seventy degrees, year-round. Guided tours depart from the entrance every half hour, beginning daily at 9 a.m.

For an extra treat, follow RR 306 to RR 32, which is a wildly twisting route known as the **Devil's Backbone.** It will lead to RR 12 and **Wimberley,** a great little resort town on the Blanco River and Cypress Creek.

LUNCH **Cypress Creek Cafe and Club,** on the Wimberley square; (512) 847-0020; www.cypresscreekcafe.com. The emphasis here is on healthful stuff, such as turkey burgers and tuna on whole-grain bread, and cappuccinos.

AFTERNOON

Spend some lazy hours milling around Wimberley's square.

Be sure to visit **The Old Mill Store** (512847-3068), which offers Mexican imports and Southwestern crafts, Jeep Collins jewelry, Texas gourmet gift items, and various contemporary art prints. Also check out **Wimberley Glass Works,** immediately south of the square on RR 12 (512- 393-3316 or 800-929-6686; www.wgw .com), a workshop and gallery that showcases exquisite blown-glass creations by local artisans.

When you're done browsing, head home to Dallas/Fort Worth due north on I-35.

If you can extend your trip, stay overnight at the **Blair House,** an elegant inn in Wimberley (100 West Spoke Hill Dr.; 512-847-1111 or 877-549-5450; www.blairhouseinn.com). There are three rooms in the main lodge, three in the Pond Cottage, two in the Honeysuckle Cottage, and another three in the Archangel Cottages. In addition, there's a spa and cooking school on-site, so you really shouldn't miss the place. Accommodations are luxurious and the amenities are lavish.

Special Events & Festivals . . . .

SEPTEMBER
Comal County Fair, New Braunfels; www.comalcountyfair.org. Nearly 120 years old, this fair offers livestock shows, horticulture exhibits, farm equipment, agricultural products, handcrafted arts, antiques, homebaked goods and food contests, as well as a professional rodeo, carnival and nightly dances.

NOVEMBER
Wurstfest, New Braunfels; (830) 625-9167; www.wurstfest.com. For a polka-dancing, wurst-feasting, beer-drinking good time; 100,000 people attend.

DECEMBER
Gruene Christmas Market Days Festival, New Braunfels; www.gru enemarketdays.com. This is the holiday version of a monthly festival (held the third weekend of each month) that brings dozens of vendors to town, selling artwork, candles, ceramics, clothing, handcrafts, furniture, glass, food, jewelry, plants, soaps and lotions, and woodwork. A visit from Santa Claus adds to the fun.

Other Recommended Restaurants & Lodgings . . . . .

NEW BRAUNFELS

Gruene Country Homestead Inn, 832 Gruene Rd.; (830) 606-0216 or (800) 238-5534; www.gruenehomesteadinn.com. Several of the twenty-seven rooms are in 1850s vintage structures of adobe, cedar, and barn wood, made by German settlers. There are also accommodations in farm houses and cottages, too. Whirlpool baths, coffeemakers, wet bars, and TVs are typical amenities.

Gruene Mansion Inn, 1275 Gruene Rd.; (830) 629-2641; www .gruenemansioninn.com. A gorgeous turn-of-the-20th-century mansion offers thirty rooms with private baths. Optional breakfast is an additional $5, and the inn's restaurant serves steaks and German cuisine at lunch and dinner.

WIMBERLEY

More options are offered through the Visit Wimberley Web site; www .visitwimberley.com.

For More Information . . . .

New Braunfels Chamber of Commerce, 390 South Seguin Ave., New Braunfels, TX 78130; (830) 625-2385 or (800) 572-2626; www.newbraunfelschamber.com.

Wimberley Chamber of Commerce, P.O. Box 12, Wimberley, TX 78676; (512) 847-2201; www.wimberley.org.

SOUTHBOUND ESCAPE *Six*

San Antonio (By Plane)
THE ALAMO CITY/2 NIGHTS

The queen city of north Texas's escapists, San Antonio is also a major vacation destination for travelers worldwide. San Antonio's international reputation and the fact that it is the nation's seventh largest city may come as a surprise to native Texans who grew up familiar with San Antonio. Whereas we once hopped into the car and showed up in SA without reservations, always finding a hotel room on the cheap, today it takes planning to get the most out of a San Antonio visit. The good news is, good deals are easy to find with a bit of research.

Missions
River Walk
Shopping
Museums
Sensational food
Multicultural heritage
Spa
Gardens

Sprawling San Antonio is a mighty tourism power to be reckoned with, drawing twenty-five million sightseers annually to its wealth of Spanish-Mexican-German-Native American-Texan culture. At any given time, thousands of conventioneers meet in the city, and thousands more leisure seekers share its bounty. There's plenty to go around, so plan ahead, make reservations, and join in the fiesta.

DAY 1/MORNING

Because San Antonio is at least a four-hour drive from Dallas/Fort Worth, your best option for a Quick Escape is to board a plane at either DFW Airport or Dallas Love Field. The flight to San Antonio

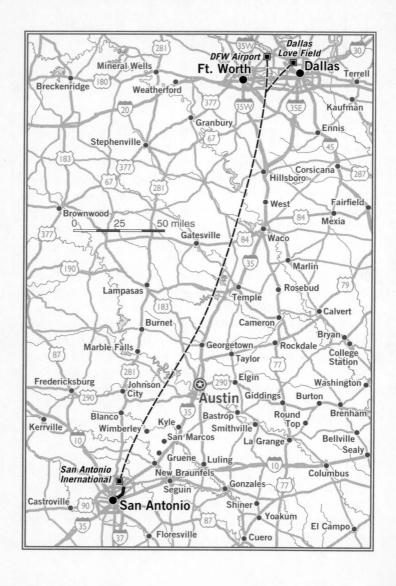

International Airport is just a little less than one hour. There, you can rent a car for your explorations.

BREAKFAST Pick up a snack at the airport to take on board with you, along with a cup of coffee or tea.

As soon as you can, stop at the visitor center facing the Alamo at 317 Alamo Plaza (800-447-3372; www.visitsanantonio.com). Guides, maps, brochures, and everything you need are there.

Now for the **Alamo,** 300 Alamo Plaza (210-225-1391; www .thealamo.org). The first of five Spanish missions established in the early 1700s, it was called Mission San Antonio de Valero. Texas history students and John Wayne film fans know the Alamo mission doubled as a fort where Davy Crockett, Jim Bowie, and William B. Travis were among the patriots who gave their lives for the Texas Revolution. For thirteen days in late February and early March of 1836, 187 men were surrounded and then crushed by the Mexican Army. See the heavy doors with bullet holes in front of what appears to be a too-tiny place for such huge history and significance. Open 9 a.m. to 5: 30 p.m. Mon through Sat and 10 a.m. to 5: 30 p.m. Sun.

If you're searching for art, consider **La Villita,** 418 Villita St. (210-207-8610). Adjacent to the River Walk, this enclave is an arts-and-crafts community of twenty-six shops for working artisans, plus three restaurants, a post office, and the Old San Antonio Exhibit. The latter houses a collection of art objects, artifacts, and symbols relevant to the Alamo-rich history of La Villita.

It's an easy walk from almost anywhere in downtown to Market Square, but you can hop the trolley from Alamo Plaza to the square, too. **Market Square,** 514 West Commerce St. (210-207-8600; www .marketsquaresa.com), is a re-created Mexican *mercado.* Here there's more shopping, this time for Mexican and Texan arts, crafts, jewelry, produce, baskets, and pottery in more than one hundred shops.

LUNCH   **Mi Tierra,** Market Square; (210) 225-1262; www.mitierra cafe.com. Homestyle Mexican food is served twenty-four hours daily at this busy restaurant. Try the green chile enchiladas and some sweets from the bakery case.

AFTERNOON

Overlooking Market Square is a nine-story tile mural titled *Spirit of Healing,* on the Houston Street side of Santa Rosa Children's Hospital. Created by nationally recognized artist Jesse Trevino, the 90-foot-by-40-foot mural is made of 150,000 hand-cut ceramic tiles, which depict a guardian angel and cross behind a child holding a dove.

While you're near the market area, you'll want to tour and photograph the recently refurbished **Spanish Governors' Palace,** 105 Plaza De Armas; (210-224-0601). Once called "the most beautiful building in San Antonio" by *National Geographic,* the National Historic Landmark was home to officials of the Spanish Province of Texas and still exhibits the original keystone over the entrance with the Spanish inscription finished in 1749. Inside are period furnishings and a cobblestone patio with fountain and lavish foliage.

Take time also to visit the **Museo Alameda,** 101 South Santa Rosa in the Market Square area (210-299-4300; www.thealameda .org). This renovated 1940s cinema was the first opened specifically to serve the Latino community in its day. Now, renovated with great care, it is the center of Latino arts and culture in San Antonio, with a Smithsonian affiliation. Stop in here to see traveling and local art exhibits, as well as to purchase artful gifts.

Leave time to roam the downtown section of the **River Walk,** too. Art galleries, clothing boutiques, gift shops, and craft stores line the more than 20 blocks of flagstone banks along the River

Walk, or Paseo del Rio, which lies beneath street level downtown and follows the river's twisting contours. Arbors of palms, olive trees, cottonwoods, cypress, and willows shade sidewalk cafes, and pots of flowers are set between doors to shops, galleries, boutiques, hotels, bistros, and watering holes.

The lines can be long on weekends to take a **river cruise tour** (210-244-5700). A thirty-five- to forty-minute affair, the cruises are a nice way to have a look at River Walk offerings and hear a little local history. Look for boarding sites along the river. Check out the Web site at www.sarivercruise.com.

DINNER **Biga on the Banks,** 203 South Saint Mary's St.; (210) 225-0722; www.biga.com. Southwestern and European ideas meet, with results such as soft-shell crab with sweet potato, oak-smoked pork loin, grilled oysters, lobster risotto, and renowned baked items from an adjoining bakery.

LODGING **Hotel Havana** at 1015 Navarro St.; (210) 222.2008; www.havanasanantonio.com. The 22,000-square-foot property, a 1914 landmark on the quiet part of the River Walk, became chic again with an early 2010 renovation that delivers vintage style from 1950s-era Cuba. Each of the twenty-seven rooms has slightly different decor, but all have hardwood floors, high ceilings, and big windows, along with iron beds, custom linens, and a minifridge filled with goodies. Each morning, guests can have breakfast baskets delivered to the room. A blend of Cuban and European style, the vividly colored straw basket opens to reveal a daily newspaper, freshly squeezed juice, and a wealth of local products, starting with El Sol Bakery's lard-free, whole wheat pan dulce in myriad forms.

After dinner, enjoy an espresso or drinks in the basement bar at the Havana, a favorite among locals. Signature drinks include mojitos, Cuba Libres, michiladas, and margaritas, or you can have a shot of mescal paired with handmade local chocolates.

DAY 2/MORNING

....

BREAKFAST Enjoy the breakfast basket at the **Havana**. If you're staying elsewhere, get breakfast at your hotel or at **Twin Sisters Bakery & Café**, 124 Broadway (210) 354-1559; www.twinsistersbakeryandcafe.com. Specialties at this hometown favorite include healthy preparations of breakfast tacos, huevos (or tofu) rancheros, and oatmeal with bananas and pecans.

Visit the latest in San Antonio's A-list attractions. At the edge of downtown, **Pearl** is the twenty-two-acre district surrounding the handsome **Pearl Brewery,** an 1883 iconic structure that serves as centerpiece for the bustling new cultural and culinary center. On Sat morning, a farmers' market brings local fresh finds to the public. But even if you don't arrive on market day, you'll find plenty to fill a morning, afternoon, or full day.

Pearl's offerings include Full Goods, a 67,000-square-foot warehouse with restaurants, the Nature Conservancy office, Twig Book Shop, and shopping at **Melissa Guerra** (www.melissaguerra .com), an 1880s-inspired Mexican *tienda* (or store) selling handcrafted leather goods, silver jewelry, Mexican tiles, bath products, antique fixtures, cookware, handcarved wooden pieces, and more.

At Pearl, you can take a Pilates or yoga class at the Synergy Studio (www.thesynergystudio.com), get a haircut with color at the Aveda Institute (www.avedaisa.com), or pick up gear for your running and hiking adventures at Run Wild Sports (www.runwildsports .com).

If you planned ahead, you can improve your cooking skills at a daylong class at the **Culinary Institute of America,** the third campus of the world's most prestigious cooking school (www.ciachef.edu/ sanantonio). The focus at this school is Latin American cuisine, of course.

LUNCH   **Il Sogno Osteria,** in the Pearl Brewery, 200 East Grayson St.; (210) 212-4843. Award winning chef Andrew Weissman follows up his insanely successful French venture, the late and much-missed La Reve, with this brilliant Italian effort. Antipasti, selected from a bar laden with perhaps fifteen choices, includes a white bean puree, roasted eggplant, and lovely salads bursting with fresh garden picks. Entrees to consider include personal pizzas and fresh fish.

AFTERNOON

Your appreciation for Spanish history in San Antonio is heightened by visiting **Mission San José,** 6701 Mission San José Dr. at Mission Road (210-932-1001). Founded two years after the Alamo, it is now the most popular of the four missions that still function as churches. The church is noted for its rare and opulent handmade Rose Window. A lively mariachi mass takes place Sunday at noon.

This mission and four others—**Mission Concepción, Mission San Francisco de la Espada, Mission San Juan Capistrano,** and **Mission San Antonio de Valero** (the Alamo)—compose the **San Antonio Missions National Historical Park.** All were part of the chain of missions established early in the 18th century by the Franciscan order of the Roman Catholic Church. Constructed primarily of adobe and native stone, the missions offer great, walled courtyards of amazing tranquility, seemingly far from the city. This collection of missions is one of the nation's few urban-area national parks. For additional tour information on the missions, contact the San Antonio Missions National Historical Park, 2202 Roosevelt Ave. (210-534-8833; www.nps.gov).

DINNER   **Liberty Bar at the Convent,** 1111 South Alamo St.; (210) 227-1187; www.liberty-bar.com. After twenty-five years in business in the same fun and funky location (the house leaned—noticeably), the Liberty is open again just south of downtown in the King William Historic District. The same menu is offered, with Southern dishes receiving European influences. Lamb sausage remains a favorite from the mesquite grill, but other treasures include the portobello sandwich with smoked gouda cheese and saffron aïoli with a side of asparagus in vinaigrette.

LODGING At **Hotel Havana** or at another fine choice, the **Ogé Inn River Walk** (pronounced oh-ZHAY) in the King William District at the River Walk and Durango; (800) 242-2770 or (210) 223-2353; www.ogeinn.com. This is an 1857 home with period antiques. Most rooms include fireplaces.

EVENING

San Antonio Rose Live (www.saroselive.com) is an oversized, two-hour homage to classic country music, playing weekends at the magnificently restored, historic **Aztec on the River,** 201 East Commerce St. (877-432-9832; www.aztecontheriver.com). The elegant old Aztec Theatre, circa 1926, has been restored to its former glory, operating now as a showplace. Look inside the three-story lobby for big wow factors, including a two-ton chandelier, Mesoamerican statues topping twelve giant columns, and a restored Wurlitzer organ.

DAY 3/MORNING

BREAKFAST Sleep in, have a late breakfast at your hotel.

Make your way back to the airport for a flight home.

There's More . . . .

Brackenridge Park, 3700 North St. Mary's St. (210-207-3000) sprawls across 343 acres that offer sunken Japanese Tea Gardens

(210-735-0663), a miniature railroad, Texas's oldest kiddie amusement park (with a 1918 carousel), paddleboats, golf, horseback riding, and a skyride. Tranquility is found on winding pebble walkways and at stone bridges, a waterfall, and pools.

San Antonio Zoo and Aquarium, 3903 North St. Mary's St. (210-734-7183; www.sazoo-aq.org), sprawls over seventy acres, occupied by 3,500 animals from more than 700 species.

Witte Museum, 3801 Broadway (210-357-1886; www.witte museum.org) is a natural and local history museum with exhibits on such subjects as dinosaurs, World War II, Japanese kimonos, and African beadwork.

Children's Museum of San Antonio, 305 East Houston St. (210-212-4453; www.sakids.org), illustrates the city's cultural diversity for ages two through ten at this hands-on facility with interactive educational exhibits.

Alamo Plaza Spa, inside the Menger Hotel, 204 Alamo Plaza (210-223-4361 or 800-345-9285; www.historicmenger.com). A two-hour treatment includes steam bath, sauna, and herbal scrub. Afterward, enjoy a drink in the bar, where it's said Teddy Roosevelt recruited his Rough Riders in 1898.

Hemis Fair Park, bordered by Alamo Street, I-37, Durango, and Market (210-207-8590). The park is at the foot of the 750-foot-tall Tower of the Americas, left over from the 1968 World's Fair. A glass elevator whisks you to the top in less than a minute, but the sky-high restaurant moves more slowly; it makes one revolution per hour. Or just explore the park's walkways, ponds, and waterfalls, and then the **Institute of Texan Cultures** (210-458-2275;

www.texancultures.com), a leading ethnic-history museum. Art, artifacts, and photographic exhibits focus on the people of twenty-eight ethnic and cultural groups in Texas; the multimedia show and museum store are also superb. Open 9 a.m. to 5 p.m. Tues through Sun.

Just south of downtown, the **King William Historic District** (on and around King William Street) is a trove of wonderful 19-century mansions built by the city's German gentry. Walking and cycling this area on spring or fall days is a pleasure long remembered, but you can have a look inside, too (www.kingwilliamassociation.org).

The **Steves Homestead,** 509 King William St. (210-227-9160; www.saconservation.org), is a century-old Victorian French Second Empire, three-story mansion on the San Antonio River furnished with period antiques. It is owned and maintained by the San Antonio Conservation Society.

For something on the bizarre side, try **Buckhorn Saloon & Museum,** 318 East Houston St. (210-247-4000; www.buckhornmuseum .com), which houses the world's largest collection of antlers, plus the Hall of Fins and Feathers, the Texas History Wax Museum, and the O. Henry House. A good family spot.

Investigate the art scene: The **McNay Art Museum,** 6000 North New Braunfels (210-824-5368; www.mcnayart.org), displays modern French works, American and European watercolors, Gothic and Flemish works, and modern Native American crafts, bronzes, and other artwork.

Also try the **San Antonio Museum of Art,** 200 West Jones Ave. (210-978-8100; www.samuseum.org). The museum is situated in an old Romanesque brewery building whose towers hold four levels of galleries reached by glass elevators. Art of the Americas, from pre-Columbian to the 20th century, and a two-and-a-half-acre sculpture garden are here, too.

Southwest School of Art & Craft, 300 Augusta St.; (210) 224-1848; www.swschool.org. Occupying the former Ursuline Order convent and girls' school, the craft center surrounds a beautiful courtyard and is the setting for classes, workshops, exhibitions, and special events. You'll find artists and craftspeople working and selling weaving, macramé, pottery, and wood carvings.

If the San Antonio Symphony is performing, it will be at the **Majestic Theatre,** 224 East Houston St.; (210) 226-5700 or (210) 226-3333; www.sasymphony.org.

See the excellent docudrama, *Alamo: The Price of Freedom,* on a six-story-tall film screen behind the Alamo in the elaborate RiverCenter Mall's IMAX Theatre. Historians play characters in this version, a more factual story than the John Wayne movie. For show schedule and ticket information, call (210) 247-4629.

Special Events & Festivals . . . .

LATE JANUARY, EARLY FEBRUARY
San Antonio Stock Show and Rodeo; (210) 225-5851. Two-week celebration of professional rodeo performances and music bill featuring country, Tejano, and rock artists.

MID-MARCH
St. Patrick's Day; (210) 497-8435 or (210) 227-4262. 10K run, one of the Southwest's largest parades, and an annual Irish

celebration of dyeing the San Antonio River a Gaelic green and renaming it the River Shannon for one day. Lots of dancing and music, too.

APRIL

Fiesta San Antonio; (210) 227-5191; www.fiesta-sa.org; begun more than a century ago, is staged now by thousands of residents and volunteers for an eleven-day run. More than 100 events include the Battle of Flowers Parade, Cavalier River Parade, Fiesta Night Parade, A Night in Old San Antonio, the king's coronation, an Alamo pilgrimage, an arts fair, and a *charreada,* or Mexican rodeo.

EARLY JUNE

Texas Folklife Festival, Institute of Texan Cultures; (210) 458-2300; http://texancultures.com. The state's largest cultural celebration honors the more than 40 cultural and ethnic groups found among Texas residents. Music, dance, theater, art and craft, and food figure prominently among merriment taking place over three days on the UTSA HemisFair Park Campus.

LATE NOVEMBER THROUGH DECEMBER

Christmas celebrations, including the River Walk Holiday Parade; Feria de Santa Cecilia & Fiestas Navideñas with mariachi music, lighting of Market Square, the blessing of the animals, and a visit by Pancho Claus; and Fiesta de las Luminarias, the lighting of thousands of candles along the River Walk, symbolizing a lighting of the way for the Holy Family's journey to Bethlehem; (210) 227-4262 or (210) 270-8700; www.visitsanantonio.com/visitors/play/festivals-events/index.aspx.

Other Recommended Restaurants and Lodgings . . . .

El Mirador, 722 South St. Mary's St.; (210) 225-9444; www.el miradorrestaurant.com. A popular meeting place for locals at breakfast and lunch, this neighborhood spot has spectacular savory soups, as well as lovely evening dishes such as red snapper in tortilla crust.

Hyatt Regency Hill Country Resort, 9800 Hyatt Resort Dr., northwest of San Antonio; (210) 647-1234 or (800) 55-HYATT; www .hillcountry.hyatt.com. This 200-acre spread was Texas's first true resort. Its mega-ranch look has woodwork and decor consistent with the pioneer period; the structure consists of native limestone prevalent in the Hill Country's German towns. Spend your time golfing, playing tennis, inner tubing on a river that winds through the property, working out or being pampered at an outdoor spa, or swimming in one of two pools. Children's and teens' programs are available.

JW Marriott San Antonio Hill Country Resort & Spa, 23808 Resort Parkway; (210) 403-3434 or (866) 882-4420; www.jwsanantonio .com. Found about a half-hour north of downtown, this is the largest JW resort with the largest spa in Texas. Covering 600 acres of rolling, rugged swells of Hill Country landscape, the resort offers 1,002 rooms, two Tournament Player's Club (TPC) golf courses, a wildlife sanctuary, abundant hiking and biking trails, a steady supply of children's programs, a half-dozen swimming pools, and six places to eat and drink. Tops are High Velocity, the mega-sports bar, and 18 Oaks, an upscale steakhouse with a fine selection of Texas wines. Check out the glass artwork by San Antonio artist Gini Garcia, as well as the proliferation of archival photography from local ranches.

The Westin La Cantera Resort, 16641 La Cantera Parkway; (210) 558-6500; www.westinlacantera.com. An exquisite destination resort that covers 300 acres in northwest San Antonio. La Cantera offers an eighteen-hole championship golf course, a lovely spa and fitness facility that overlooks the resort's five terraced pools, and several restaurants, including the outstanding Francesca's at Sunset, which has a "Nuevo Latino" menu created by Mark Miller of Coyote Cafe fame. This top-notch resort has marvelous landscaping and makes perfect use of Texas's native limestone.

For More Information . . . .

San Antonio Convention and Visitors Bureau, 203 South St. Mary's St., second floor, San Antonio, TX 78205; (800) 447-3372; www .visitsanantonio.com.

SOUTHBOUND ESCAPE *Seven*

Bandera, Lost Maples, and Boerne (By Plane)

DUDE RANCHES AND HILL COUNTRY GLORY/2 NIGHTS

Bandera is known as the Cowboy Capital of the World not just for its cattle drive and ranching heritage, but also for the record number of National Rodeo Champions who have called the town home. But what travelers most enjoy is access to the cowboy life, available at several dude ranches along

> Cowboy breakfasts
> Trail rides
> Spelunking
> River tubing
> Hiking
> Spa luxuries

the cypress and live oak-laden banks of the Medina River. Rugged countryside—marked by Native American, Mexican, Polish, and Western influences—about 45 miles west of San Antonio provides the ultimate escape terrain, even if just for a weekend. There's also a nearby stand of big tooth maples, oddly distant from all others on the continent, and Boerne, a Hill Country town noted for its deep German heritage.

DAY 1/MORNING

From Dallas/Fort Worth, the fastest way southwest to Bandera is via a quick (just less than an hour) flight to San Antonio. Board an early flight from DFW Airport or Dallas Love Field, grabbing breakfast at the airport. In San Antonio, hop in your rental car, drive west on I-410 and north on Texas 16 for the 55-mile ride to Bandera.

The desire to play cowboy and cowgirl for a weekend or week is what draws people to Bandera's ranches, many of which have

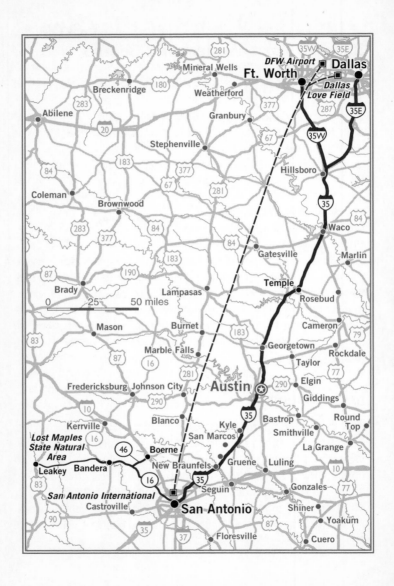

been family lodging businesses since the 1930s. Each of the ranches here affords accommodations for families or couples in bunkhouses or cabins. Some ranches offer complete schedules full of activities, such as horseback riding and hayrides, trick-roping and snake-handling demonstrations, rodeos, country-western dancing, chuckwagon meals on the trail, golfing, swimming, fishing, and inner tubing on the Medina River. Others let guests think up their own amusements.

Check into a ranch, such as **Dixie Dude Ranch,** 9 miles south of town on RR 1077 (830-796- 7771 or 800-375-9255; www .dixieduderanch.com). A family operation for seventy-plus years, this 800-acre spread is rough and comfortable at the same time. The main lodge is a homey place where guests make friends from all over the globe during fried-chicken suppers, poolside cookouts, and Saturday-night barbecues. The ranch hands—especially good at matching riders with mounts—lead trail rides through a wild terrain and point out historic sites along the way.

A really different ranch experience is found at **Hill Country Equestrian Lodge,** a place for really learning how to ride a horse or to enjoy skills you already have while roaming the adjacent 5,500-acre Hill Country State Park. Nobody mounts one of the beautiful, gentle horses at Hill Country Equestrian Lodge without at least a short riding lesson from ranch co-owner Dianne Lindig. A lifelong equestrienne and former fitness instructor, Lindig's calm personality and obvious expertise suit both novice and veteran riders. Although many guests come to the lodge (about 10 miles from Bandera via RR 1077; 830-796-7950; www.hillcountryequestlodge .com) specifically to improve their riding skills at one of Lindig's workshops or in private lessons—some even bring their own horses, which Lindig boards in her stables—there are plenty who have no intention of getting in a saddle, and that's fine. An ample list of simple distractions keeps guests amused.

Trails found on the ranch and in the adjacent 5,500-acre state park offer varying degrees of difficulty for hikers and mountain bikers. Lindig says guests can bring their own bikes or use the ranch's, and that competitive bikers even go to train there. Others love roaming around looking for flint, quartz, and sandstone rocks, as well as fossils. Lindig says business is growing also among bird-watchers who come to the ranch to put the year-round resident mountain jays on their life lists. You can hang out in the Jacuzzi or visit Sea World, about forty-five minutes away. When the afternoons are blistering hot, you can play cards in your pretty, comfortable cedar-and-limestone cabin, one of several built on the oak-studded swells covering the old Britsch family ranch, which operated as a sheep and goat ranch for more than a century.

Guests at the lodge do as they please, Lindig doesn't push structured activities on you. You can cook in your cabin's kitchen—breakfast makings are provided, and you can pick up groceries in Bandera for lunch and supper. This is a great place to sit on the porch in silence to watch the sun come and go, and you can ask Lindig to bring in a masseuse or facial therapist.

LUNCH If not at your ranch, try **OST**, 305 Main St.; (830) 796-3836. It is named for the Old Spanish Trail on which Bandera lies. Good choices include chicken-fried steak, biscuits and gravy, Mexican food, and grilled steaks.

AFTERNOON

Either ride and swim at the ranch, or spend a couple of hours perusing a funky collection of antiques and junk at the **Frontier Times Museum,** 506 13th St. (830-796-3864). There are more than 40,000 items, including bottles from Judge Roy Bean's saloon, 500 bells from around the world, antique firearms and saddles, and spearheads and arrowheads.

About 5 blocks southwest of the museum, see **St. Stanislaus Catholic Church and Convent Cemetery** at the corner of Cypress and 8th Streets. Bandera's Polish roots date from 1855, when sixteen Polish families immigrated to the little town to work at the mill, and their church was built in 1876. An interesting note: This is the second-oldest Polish Catholic church in the United States.

Back on Main Street, in front of the courthouse, you'll find a bronze monument that names Bandera as the Cowboy Capital of the World and lists the many National Rodeo Champions from here. Also downtown, see **Bunkhouse Leather,** 1207 Cedar St.; (800) 861-3690; www.bunkhousesaddlery.com. Here, you can see saddles being repaired and sometimes even a horse being brought in so that the right saddle can be chosen to fit mount and rider.

Over time, Bandera's shopping has grown in depth and appeal. In historic buildings in the town's center, you'll find stores selling jeans, boots, and hats, as well as local crafts.

Duffers will be happy to know there are two eighteen-hole golf courses, both at Bandera ranches. At **Flying L Guest Ranch,** 1 mile from town, off TX 173 South (800-292-5134 or 830-796-8466; www.flyingl.com), there's a championship course and driving range.

If you need to cool off after a day in town, plan a late afternoon inner-tubing or canoeing trip on the Medina River. Check out the rentals at **Medina River Company,** next to the Longhorn Saloon on TX 16 North (830-796-3600), or at one of the other outfitters the local tourism office includes on its Web site, www.banderacowboy-capital.com.

DINNER   Back at the ranch. If you're staying at Hill Country Equestrian Lodge, buy groceries in town for supper in your cabin.

After dinner, visit the legendary honky-tonk **Arkey Blues Silver Dollar Bar,** 308 Main St. in Bandera (830-796-8826). This sawdust-covered beer joint features live Texas music. Even those who don't drink or dance should take a peek inside. Other Bandera spots for live music include the Longhorn Saloon, Blue Gene's, and the Bandera Saloon.

Another hot spot for live music and country-western culture is the **11th Street Cowboy Bar,** 307 11th St., Bandera; (830) 796-4849; www.11thstreetcowboybar.com. There's a 5,200-square-foot dance floor, four barbecue pits, four bars, two stages, covered and open seating outside, and a Sunday jam session.

DAY 2/MORNING

| BREAKFAST | At the ranch. |

Either play the day away at the ranch or plan a trip. Head west on TX 16 and RR 337 for the especially breathtaking Hill Country drives in the Leakey-Utopia-Vanderpool area. Here on the region's western edge, the Frio, Nueces, and Sabinal Rivers create vivid shaded canyons from which hills and mesas rise between 1,500 and 2,400 feet. The specific drives from Leakey that attract photographers, painters, and other artists of the soul are RR 337 West to Camp Wood, past wooded rises and lonely green valleys colored purple in spring with mountain laurel, and RR 337 East into Bandera County to Vanderpool, then north on RR 187 to glorious **Lost Maples State Natural Area** (830-966-3413; www.tpwd.state.tx.us).

Dedicated fall foliage fans are familiar with these woods, which aren't exactly lost, despite the name. The big tooth maples found here are such a long way from others of their kind—which are scattered over several western states and northern New Mexico—that it seems they took a wrong turn somewhere. Because their shallow roots are susceptible to damage by soil compaction, visiting hikers/walkers are urged to stay on marked paths in the park. Fall color, which includes vivid yellows, oranges, and reds that peak in early November, brings crowds in droves on the weekends; if you can visit during the week, you'll be glad. Indeed the park abounds in flora and fauna. There are ninety plant families, including an escarpment chokecherry and a Texas ash that have been nominated to the American Forestry Association's Big Tree program for consideration as national champs. Bird-watchers will delight in the rare golden-cheeked warbler. The park has campsites with water and electricity, picnic areas, restrooms, showers, and primitive camping areas, the latter reached by almost 11 miles of hiking and backpacking trails.

Just south of Lost Maples State Natural Area is the **Lone Star Motorcycle Museum,** 36517 TX 187 North, Vanderpool (830-966-6103; www.lonestarmotorcyclemuseum.com). Open only on weekends, this impressive collection of bikes offers models dating back to 1910. There's a good cafe on-site, too.

LUNCH Picnic in the park, or try **Lost Maples Cafe,** Main in Utopia; (830) 966-2221; www.lostmaplescafe.com. A friendly diner with excellent barbecue, chicken-fried steak, and burgers. Or check out **Ace Café,** inside the Lone Star Motorcycle Museum, above, for Aussie pies, an Australian specialty, as well as burgers, salads, and pecan pie.

AFTERNOON

Continue the scenic drives, or find a spot to swim in the pretty Frio River.

A lovely place to play in the Frio is **Garner State Park,** just off US 83 (830-232-6132; www.tpwd.state.tx.us), situated mid-way between Concan, a tiny burg settled about 1840, and Leakey. Spreading over 1,420 acres along the Frio and on the far edge of the Edwards Plateau, Garner is a delight with stone-and-timber cabins, miniature golf course, showers, grocery store, and exceptional hiking.

More than a few day-trippers have happened along the Frio and decided to stay for a while. If you find yourself in this boat, check out the digs at **Neal's Lodges** at Concan (830-232-6118; www.nealslodges.com), with sixty comfortable cabins, dining rooms, general store, game room, riding stables, and post office. Another favorite is **River Haven Cabins** on the Frio (830-232-5400; www.riverhavencabins.com).

DINNER Back at the ranch, or have burgers, steaks, and wine at **Brick's Restaurant** 1205 Main St. in Bandera; (830) 460-3200.

LODGING At the ranch or Hill Country Equestrian Lodge.

DAY 3/MORNING

BREAKFAST Another big cowboy spread at the ranch.

Say bye to the ranch and drive east on TX 46 about 20 miles from Bandera to Boerne, pronounced BURN-ee. Day-trippers from San Antonio, just 30 miles southeast, are hereabouts, browsing through the creaky old antiques shops—packed with great little finds—or at one of the pleasant restaurants in town. Two of Texas's fascinating caves are right here; the larger is **Cascade Caverns,** 3 miles south on I-10 to Cascade Caverns Road (830-755-8080; www

.cascadecaverns.com), with a 90-foot-high interior waterfall crashing from an underground stream. Smaller and far less commercial (and not open regularly) is **Cave Without A Name** (830-537-4212). Drive 6 miles on FR 474 East to Kreutzberg Road and 5 miles in the only direction possible along this road to the cave. It is 98 percent active and is enormous, filled with stalagmites and stalactites, soda straws, strips of bacon, gnomes, and all sorts of mushrooming formations.

Make time to just goof around in the town of Boerne, established in 1848 as a German farm commune named Tusculum. As more German settlers arrived, they renamed their town for German political journalist Ludwig Börne.

Check out the **Kuhlmann-King Historical House,** 402 East Blanco St.; (830) 249-2030. Historic documents are housed in the Archives Building, adjacent to the two-story home built in the late 1880s by German physicist William Kuhlmann. It's open on Sun afternoon only.

LUNCH　　　　**Peach Tree Cafe,** 448 South Main St.; (830) 249-8583. Tucked into a cute little Victorian house, this sweet dining room serves lunch specials of meat loaf or chicken breast with walnut crust, chicken and spinach salads, shrimp gumbo, quiche, and excellent cheese rolls, peach cobbler, and pecan-fudge cake. Or try the **Limestone Grill** at **Ye Kendall Inn,** 128 West Blanco St.; (800) 364-2138; www.yekendallinn.com. At this lovely restaurant inside one of Texas's favorite restored inns, try panko-crusted Thai shrimp, seasonal soups, and crème brûlée. There's a nice wine list, too.

AFTERNOON

Head back to San Antonio for your flight home.

There's More . . . .

Apple orchards, in and around Medina, known as the Apple Capital of Texas. In spring the trees burst with delicate pink and white blossoms, and in summer you can pick your own apples in the orchards open to the public. Medina is 13 miles northwest of Bandera via Texas 16. **The Apple Store** (830-589-2202) features fresh apples and apple products.

Fishing, sailing, scuba diving, and **waterskiing** are available at **Medina Lake.** Anglers love the bass, catfish, crappie, and white bass in the crystal waters of the 5,575-acre impoundment on the Medina River. The lake is 23 miles southeast of Bandera via TX 46 East and FR 1283 South.

Hill Country State Park, 10 miles west of Bandera via FR 1077; (830) 796-4413. There are 34 miles of spectacular equestrian trails in this undeveloped spread of 5,400 acres, popular also for primitive camping, backpacking, and mountain biking.

Go to the Friday night rodeo at **Twin Elm Guest Ranch** (830-796-3628 or 888-567-3049) or to the Saturday night rodeo at **BR Lightning Ranch** (830-535-4096). On Labor Day Weekend, there's bull riding during Celebrate Bandera, below.

Wildlife, throughout Bandera County. Exotics include axis deer, small but colorful blackbuck antelope, palm-antlered fallow deer, Russian boar, hogs, and wild turkey. Call ahead to check out hunting options at (800) 364-3833.

On the prettiest days, **Guadalupe River State Park,** TX 46 and Park Road 31, 16 miles east of Boerne (830-438-2656), beckons with

1,900 acres of cypress, limestone bluffs, and natural rapids on the benevolent Guadalupe River. A good spot for canoeing, fishing, hiking, camping, and nature study.

Special Events & Festivals . . . .

MID-JUNE
Berges Fest, a three-day German festival, Boerne; (830) 249-8000; www.bergesfest.com. An old-fashioned street party lasting three days, this celebration of German heritage includes the coronation of Miss Berges Fest, a parade, food and craft vendors, live music, and dancing.

EARLY SEPTEMBER
Celebrate Bandera on Labor Day Weekend is now recognized as one of the top 100 Western events in the United States by *American Cowboy Magazine;* www.celebratebandera.com.

Other Recommended Restaurants & Lodgings . . . . .

BANDERA
Backroads Texas, www.backroadstexas.net, is a reliable reservations service representing several properties in Bandera County.

Flying L Guest Ranch, 566 Flying L Dr., Bandera; (830) 460-3001; www.flyingl.com. Perfect for families and all kinds of groups, this busy ranch has plentiful horseback riding, rodeo events, a full-size water park, eighteen-hole golf course, a ghost town, live music and dancing, and campfire activities.

Running R Ranch, 9 miles west of town via FR 1077; (830) 796-3984; www.rrranch.com. Fourteen Western-style cabins with kitchenettes, bunkhouse for six, horseback riding, swimming pool, and pool table.

BOERNE
Boerne Sunday House, 911 South Main St.; (830) 249-9563 or (800) 633-7339; www.boernevistro.com. Fourteen rooms with antique furnishings, TV, phones; adjacent restaurant.

Po-Po Family Restaurant, 7 miles north of Boerne via I-10 at exit 533; (830) 537-4194; www.poporestaurant.com. Since 1929, this bustling, popular lunch and dinner place has been a great bet for grilled steaks, fried chicken livers, broiled fish, and good service. You'll be amazed at the collection of more than 1,600 plates covering the walls.

LEAKEY-VANDERPOOL
Foxfire Log Cabins, 1 mile south of Lost Maples; (830) 966-2200; www.foxfirecabins.com. Seven antiques-furnished log cabins along the Sabinal River, as well as numerous vacation houses in the surrounding area.

Frio Canyon Lodge, on US 83 in Leakey; (830) 232-6800; www.friocanyonlodge.com. An old-fashioned tourist court motel updated with a delightful stone-and-wood rustic appeal. The beautiful swimming pool is surrounded by big pots of blooming plants, and the restaurant serves soups, salads, steaks, and fish.

The Lodge at Lost Maples, RR 337 between Vanderpool and Leakey; (877) 216-5627; www.lostmaplescabins.com. Cabins here have fireplaces, hardwood floors, full kitchen, heat and air-conditioning; the sensational scenery is matched by breakfasts that feature pecan twists, peach muffins, and chocolate muffins.

For More Information . . . .

Bandera Convention and Visitors Bureau, P.O. Box 171, Bandera, TX 78003; (800) 364-3833; www.banderacowboycapital.com. This office provides good maps for finding places on back roads.

Boerne Chamber of Commerce, 1 Main Plaza, Boerne, TX 78006; (830) 249-8000 or (888) 842-8080; www.boerne.org.

SOUTHBOUND ESCAPE *Eight*
Kerrville and Comfort (By Plane)
ON THE RANCH AND IN TOWN/2 NIGHTS

Cowboy artwork

Handmade jewelry

Scenic Guadalupe

River drives

Exotic beasts

Antiques shopping

Bats

Country cooking

The first night of this escape is spent in Kerrville, the Kerr County seat and largest city in the Texas Hill Country. Kerrville acts also as the region's spiritual epicenter; it rests astride the Guadalupe River and supplies everything needed for an escape, such as clean air, clear water, limestone bluffs, green valleys, generous ranchlands, gratifying foods, and comfortable rest.

Night two of the getaway is just down the road a piece, in a town most appropriately called Comfort. Just inside Kendall County, the tiny hamlet was settled in 1854 by freethinking German intellectuals who, like so many Europeans, made homes in the New World, away from religious and political persecution. The Comfort settlers, in fact, waited four decades before establishing a church.

DAY 1/MORNING

This Quick Escape comes that way only if you fly to San Antonio, then drive into the countryside west of the city. Board an early-morning flight from DFW Airport or Dallas Love Field and rent a car in the San Antonio airport. Pick up breakfast to-go at one of the airport dining courts before your flight to enjoy on the ride, which takes a bit less than an hour.

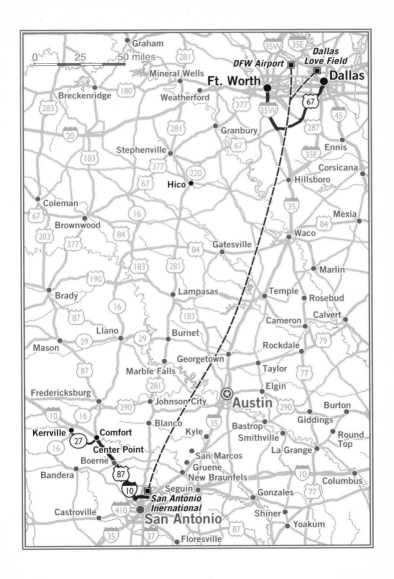

Once you're in your rental car and leaving San Antonio, you'll head west on I-410 and then north on US 87 for the hour-long drive to Kerrville. Once you're in Kerrville, there are two places to see for your orientation. The first is the **Museum of Western Art,** 1550 Bandera Hwy (830-896-2553; http://museumofwesternart .com). Likely the only American museum dedicated to the work of a single group of living artists, the museum features the paintings and sculptures of about thirty members, some of whom are considered the country's foremost proponents of Western American Realism. The building itself—one of the last works of architect O'Neil Ford—is also artistic, a mastery of light Mexican brick in *boveda* domes that need no supporting forms or wiring. Open Mon through Sat 9 a.m. to 5 p.m. Closed Sun and Mon.

LUNCH **Francisco's,** 201 Earl Garrett; (830) 257-2995; www.fran ciscos-restaurant.com. Diners feel transported to Mexico City within this art-filled, renovated historical building, where an industrious kitchen turns out jewels such as chalupa Veracruzana and lovely pastas and steaks. Open for dinner also.

AFTERNOON

Kerrville is well known for the jewelry from **James Avery Craftsman,** Harper Road just north of I-10 (830-895-1122; jamesavery.com). The creator of famous gold and silver rings and pendants—often bearing doves, crosses, and animals—Avery began making jewelry in his Kerrville garage. Now his stores are across Texas, Louisiana, Oklahoma, and Tennessee, and his mail-order business is enormous. A factory shop is open at his headquarters, and tours to see the crafting process are offered.

Fond of the outdoors and wild beasts? Then you'll enjoy an afternoon at the hilly and terribly scenic **Kerr Wildlife Management**

Area (on FR 1340 between Hunt and TX 41; 830-238-4483; www
.tpwd.state.tx.us), where state parks' efforts focus on proper range
management of native species, including white-tailed deer and turkeys. Pick up a map at the front gate for the free, self-guided car
tour and bring field glasses for spotting such birds as the black-
capped vireo and the golden-cheeked warbler.

An hour or so before sunset, take a drive west from Kerrville on
RR 1340, which winds its way through the scenic burgs of Ingram
and Hunt. The ribbon of road twists and turns, repeatedly crossing the Guadalupe River, etching its way past summer cottages
and boys' and girls' camps and through deer-hunting country. In
the middle of one field, you'll be amazed by a Stonehenge replica
(nicknamed **Bubbahenge**); it's on private ranchland, but a walking
path is provided from the road for a closer look. Several shops and
galleries are in Ingram, as well.

A good map of this area, with details on topography, is available from the **West Kerr County Chamber of Commerce** (830-367-
4322; www.wkcc.com).

In the evening from May through Aug, enjoy watching a play
or musical under the stars at **Point Theatre,** TX 39 West in Ingram
(830-367-5121; www.hcaf.com). Typical presentations on this
long-established stage include Neil Simon's *Rumors* and the comedy *Cheaper by the Dozen* as well as favorite musicals such as *Man
of La Mancha* and *Bye Bye Birdie*.

DINNER **Cowboy Steak House,** 416 Main St., Kerrville; (830) 896-
5688; www.cowboysteakhouse.com. It doesn't get more Texan that at this longtime
favorite. Appetizers include fried mushrooms, grilled shrimp, stuffed jalapeños,
quail, and bacon-wrapped scallops, and entrees run the gamut from a big por-
terhouse, filet mignon, and rib eye to rack of lamb, steak and lobster, and broiled
liver and onions. If you just want a barbecue plate or a burger, those are on the
menu, too.

LODGING   **Inn of the Hills Conference Resort,** 1001 Junction Hwy.; (830) 895-5000 or (800) 292-5690; www.innofthehills.com. In this complex, with motel rooms, suites, and condo-apartments surrounded by pretty landscaping, there are many diversions: four pools, kids' games and activities, three restaurants, an exercise facility with sauna and whirlpool, bowling lanes, putting green, bike and boat rentals, fishing in a stocked lake, and lighted tennis courts.

DAY 2/MORNING

BREAKFAST   Inn of the Hills Conference Resort.

Now it's off to the **Y.O. Ranch,** about a half hour west on I-10 and then TX 41 (830-640-3222 or 800-967-2624; www.yoranch .com). The ranch is run by the descendants of Charles Schreiner, who became a Texas Ranger at age sixteen and later served as a captain in the Civil War. He's the reason Kerrville and the Texas longhorn breed remain vibrant Texas assets. Today the Y.O. consists of 40,000 acres of the 550,000 that Schreiner acquired in 1880. It is home to roughly 10,000 animals representing more than fifty species, including wildebeest, oryx, addax, Japanese sika, aoudad, black buck antelope, ostrich, giraffe, zebra, Watusi cattle, Texas longhorn, and Spanish goats. Modern-day Schreiners are heavily involved in conservation, which is shared in ranch programs for children. Visitors must make reservations to take an extensive bus tour to see animals, and camera safaris are regularly scheduled. Horseback rides can be arranged, as can a lineup of other activities, including archery and hiking.

LUNCH   Book ahead for the **Y.O. Ranch's** chuckwagon spread, typically a ranch hand's fill of roast beef, mashed potatoes, green beans, rolls, and banana pudding. Tour and lunch together are $32.95 for adults and half-price for kids.

AFTERNOON

From Kerrville head east for a lazy drive along TX 27 to the town of Comfort. Take an hour or so to ramble along High Street, particularly the 800 block, to revel in a wonderfully intact 19th-century business district filled with wonderful shops. The Chamber of Commerce office, at 7th and High Streets (830-995-3131), has free, helpful maps that detail a wealth of historical and architectural points of interest. Shoppers will especially enjoy **Comfort Common, 717 High St.** (830-995-3030; www.comfortcommon.com), a bevy of antiques and gift boutiques in the old Ingenhuett-Faust Hotel.

And while on High Street, stroll down to see the **Treue Der Union Monument,** between 3rd and 4th Streets. This marker honors some of the liberal-minded German settlers of Comfort who joined the Union forces in the Civil War. This probably is the only Union monument in a Confederate state, other than those in military cemeteries.

Comfort is known, too, for being batty: the **Hygieostatic Bat Roost,** 1½ miles east on FR 473, was a 1918 research experiment. Seventy-five years later, the bats still use it. Sunset is the time to watch for them here and at the **Old Railroad Tunnel,** 14 miles north via FR 473 and Old Highway 9, where several thousand bats live in a tunnel abandoned in 1942.

DINNER **Cypress Creek Inn,** TX 27 at Cypress Creek Bridge; (830) 995-3977; www.cypresscreekinn.com. Open since 1952, the inn's home cooking pleases with traditional fare, such as pork chops, meat loaf, baked chicken, liver and onions, chicken-fried steak, and homemade pies. Open daily for lunch and Wed through Sat for dinner.

LODGING At your Kerrville hotel or at **Meyer Bed and Breakfast,** 845 High St.; (830) 995-2304 or (800) 364-2138; www.meyerbedandbreakfast.com. Known for years as Gast Haus Lodge, this historic, 1870s hostelry has nine suites and rooms with private baths, some kitchenettes, antique furnishings, a swimming pool, and fishing behind the complex in Cypress Creek. A big country breakfast is served. The main building was a stage stop in Comfort's earliest days.

DAY 3/MORNING

BREAKFAST At your Kerrville hotel or at **Meyer Bed and Breakfast.**

Before starting home, take a short detour to **Camp Verde,** 17 miles west of Comfort via TX 27 and then RR 480. Barely a wide spot in the road, Camp Verde only has forty residents but a Texas-size heritage. At its heart is **Camp Verde General Store,** intersection of TX 173 and RR 480 (830-634-7722; www.campverdegeneralstore .com), in continual operation since 1857. Inside you'll find great souvenirs, such as Hill Country jams and jellies, wood carvings, books, and home decor items. The store has a camel theme, recalling an 1856 military experiment in which U.S. Secretary of War Jefferson Davis established Camp Verde to house his new camel corps for the U.S. Army. He tried to prove camels would be useful for transportation across the arduous west to Fort Yuma, California. While the experiment was somewhat successful, the fort was commandeered by Confederate forces in 1861, when the Civil War erupted, and the camels were allowed to die or wander away.

For another intriguing glimpse into the past, point the car northeast on FR 490 and travel 7 miles to the burg of Center Point. On the southern edge of town, find the **Center Point Community Cemetery.** It has the distinction of containing more gravesites of Rangers, the legendary law enforcement group founded in 1823 by Stephen F. Austin, than any other Texas town.

Head back to the San Antonio airport for your flight home.

There's More . . . .

Kerrville-Schreiner State Park, 2385 Bandera Hwy.; (830) 257-5392. The park is on 500 acres along the Guadalupe River with swimming, fishing, boating, hiking, camping, and picnicking.

Riverside Nature Center, 150 Francisco Lemos, Kerrville; (830) 257-4837; www.riversidenaturecenter.org. Flowering gardens, butterfly gardens, herb gardens, and a lovely visitor center with gift shop offer good insight to native plants.

Scott Schreiner Municipal Golf Course, Country Club at Sidney Baker; (830) 257-4982. Eighteen holes on hilly terrain, pro shop, golf carts, putting greens; showers and lockers.

Special Events & Festivals . . . .

MID-APRIL
Cowboy Artists of America Roundup, (830) 896-2553; http://museumofwesternart.com. A weekend-long show and sale of cowboy artwork includes a chuck-wagon lunch and an art auction.

LATE MAY-EARLY JUNE
Kerrville Folk Festival, (830) 257-3600; www.kerrville-music.com. Eighteen days of musical events at Quiet Valley Ranch.

LATE AUGUST-EARLY SEPTEMBER
Kerrville Wine & Music Festival, (830) 257-3600; www.kerrville-music.com. Labor Day weekend tradition, with performances by songwriters and entertainers from around the nation, as well as wine-tasting events.

OCTOBER

Comfort Village Antique Show, (830) 995-3111. Folks come to town to show and sell antiques, including those in Early Country, Gardening, Architectural, Southwestern/Indian, American Oak, Blue Willow, and Stoneware styles. Baskets and textiles are included.

Other Recommended Restaurants & Lodgings . . . . .

COMFORT

The Haven River Inn, 105 Highway 473; (830) 995-3834; www .havenriverinn.com. A peaceful setting on 23 acres of land along the Guadalupe River, where you can float in a tube on the river, fish or just sit under the pecan trees. Stay in one of 14 rooms in the main house (13 with private baths). There's a third-floor, three-bedroom/two-bath suite with living, dining and kitchen areas, too.

HUNT

Casa del Rio Cottage, TX 39; (830) 238-4424; www.casadelrio-cottage.com. Attractive stone cottage on the Guadalupe bank has equipped kitchenette, full bath, cable TV, air-conditioning and heat, as well as picnic and barbecue facilities.

INGRAM

Lazy Hills Guest Ranch, west from Kerrville on TX 27, just past Ingram; (830) 367-5600. Guest rooms; horseback riding, tennis, swimming, fishing, hot tub, family-style dining in beautiful hilly setting.

NEAR KERRVILLE

Hill Country Vacation Rentals, in Hunt (830-377-2867; www.hill countryvacationrentals.com), represents cottages, B&Bs, and inns.

Welfare Café, 223 Waring-Welfare Rd., between Boerne and Kerrville; (830) 537-3700; www.welfaretexas.com. Open Thurs through Sun, this unlikely find is worth seeking out for exceptional cooking. The menu includes such pleasures as roasted poblano chile-goat cheese gratin, Cajun boudin spring rolls, smoked pork tenderloin, and a variety of schnitzels. A good wine list is offered.

For More Information . . . .

Comfort Chamber of Commerce, 7th and High Streets, Comfort, TX 78013; (830) 995-3131; www.comfortchamberofcommerce.com.

Kerrville Convention and Visitors Bureau, 1200 Sidney Baker, Kerrville, TX 78028; (830) 896-1155 or (800) 221-7958; www.kerrvilletx.com.

SOUTHBOUND ESCAPE *Nine*
The Fredericksburg Route
(By Car or Plane)
BAVARIAN RETREAT/2 NIGHTS

German food
Native stone architecture
Art and antiques shopping
Historic lodgings
Archaeology
Scenic drives
Wineries
Rivers and hilly terrain

The search for serenity has led travelers to Fredericksburg since 1846, when German settlers arrived to form the second colony under the Society for the Protection of German Immigrants in Texas and named their place for Prince Frederick of Prussia. The pioneers wrestled with disease and starvation to establish their new home, free from religious and political tyranny, in lands spread with cedar, mesquite, six kinds of oak, elm, hackberry, cottonwood, sycamore, willow, and pecan trees.

In the spring, visitors head to this Hill Country gem to revel in a multitude of Texas wildflowers. The indigo-hued bluebonnet, the state flower, forms heavy quilts on field after field, roadsides, and hillsides, so watch for lines of cars pulled to the highway shoulders as visitors stop to shoot rolls of film against farmland backdrops of cattle, sheep, goats, pigs, and horses. Summertime brings an abundant peach crop to the groves and markets in and around Fredericksburg.

En route, you'll visit Johnson City, the town where Lyndon B. Johnson, thirty-sixth president of the United States, was raised. The town has grown in recent years to offer plenty of antiques shopping, dining, and B&B stays for people who want something less busy than nearby Fredericksburg.

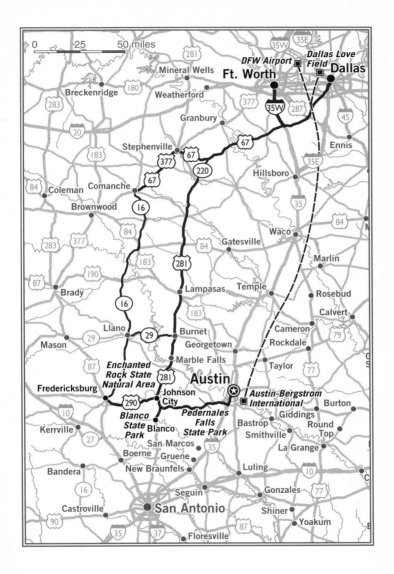

Fredericksburg, home to more than 350 bed-and-breakfast stays and guesthouses, offers good choices for anyone looking for historic architecture, food and wine, shopping, and nearby hiking.

DAY 1/MORNING

The drive to Fredericksburg, which follows lovely country highways, such as US 67, 281, and TX 16, is roughly a four-hour effort. You're better off taking a quick (about 30-minute) flight from DFW Airport or Dallas Love Field to Austin. There, rent a car for the hourlong drive west via US 290 to Fredericksburg, a route that passes through Johnson City. Pick up breakfast at the airport before boarding your flight.

From Austin, you'll want to stop first in Johnson City, the childhood home to President Lyndon B. Johnson, the only native Texan to serve in that office (Eisenhower was born in Denison but raised in Kansas; George H. W. Bush lived in Midland and Houston as an adult but was raised back East; and George W. Bush was born in New Haven, Connecticut, but moved to Texas with his family at age two).

Turn west on US 290, also called Main Street (which bears signs that read Pearl Harbor Memorial Highway), and allow yourself an hour, minimum, to look around town. The native stone construction seen throughout the Hill Country, particularly in towns where Germans settled, is also found in Johnson City.

The LBJ Boyhood Home, Avenue G at 9th St. (830-868-7128; www.nps.gov/lyjo/planyourvisit/boyhoodhome.htm), is part of the LBJ National Historical Park. Now restored, the simple house became home to LBJ in 1913 (who was born in the Gillespie Country countryside), when he was five. The visitor center sits across the street; from there you can walk on a trail a few blocks west to the Johnson Settlement, where the president's ancestors lived and farmed. There's a complex of renovated buildings—including LBJ's grandfather's log house—that provides historical information on the land's early uses and today's farming and ranching practices.

Drive 14 miles west from Johnson City on US 290 to reach the **LBJ State Park** (www.tpwd.state.tx.us/spdest/findadest/parks /lyndon_b_johnson) and the rest of **LBJ National Historical Park** (830-868-7128 or 830-644-2252; www.nps.gov/lyjo/index.htm), near the town of Stonewall. The state park's visitor center has exhibits and slide shows, and the park itself offers wildlife displays, hiking paths, tennis courts, a baseball field, a picnic area, and a large swimming pool. This park runs the **Sauer-Beckmann Living Historical Farm,** a reconstructed pioneer farm. Staff at the farm help illustrate early Hill Country life and work.

At the state park visitor center, you can pick up a free permit and CD and drive onto the ranch in your private auto—the Texas White House is now open for tours ($2), too, to see where LBJ retired (and died) and where Lady Bird lived out her life, too. On the ranch property, you'll see the reconstructed LBJ birthplace, the Junction School (where LBJ was educated), the family cemetery, a cattle show barn, and the airplane hangar that now serves as a visitor center.

LUNCH   **Hill Country Cupboard,** at the intersection of US 281 and US 290 (830-868-4625; www.hillcountrycupboard.com), specializes in chicken-fried steak, country fried pork chops, barbecue, and burgers.

AFTERNOON

If you're taking your time before going on to Fredericksburg, drive 14 miles south of Johnson City on US 281 to the town of Blanco. Settled in 1853, the charming hamlet of 1,600 is for wanderers who really want to be away from everything.

The town's showpiece is the old **Blanco County Courthouse,** built in 1885, a lasting, excellent example of Second Empire-style architecture. When the Blanco County seat was moved to Johnson City in 1891, this beautiful masterpiece became a forgotten relic. The courthouse, which recently underwent a mammoth restoration, was added to the National Register of Historic Places in 1990.

Surrounding the courthouse square are delightful antiques stores, art galleries, flea markets, restaurants, and artisans, all within historic buildings. For walking or driving tour maps and more information, call the **Blanco Chamber of Commerce** (830-833-5101; www.blancochamber.com).

Or continue from Johnson City on US 290, west of the state park and LBJ Ranch, about 20 miles to Fredericksburg. En route, you may want to stop at **Grape Creek Vineyard,** 10 miles east of Fredericksburg in the burg of Stonewall (830-644-2710 or 800-950-7392; www.grapecreek.com). Estate-bottled varietals and blends of cabernet sauvignon, chardonnay, and sauvignon blanc are produced under the Texas Hill Country appellation at this vineyard. On-site you'll find an underground cellar, a gift shop, a beautiful, Tuscan-style tasting room, and guided tours.

The best-known of the Fredericksburg-area wineries is **Becker Vineyards,** 64 Becker Farms Rd., Stonewall (830-644-2681; www.beckervineyards.com). Stories about this accomplished wine producer have appeared in the *Wine Spectator* and on the Fine Living Channel. What's more, these wines have been served at the White House. Visit the tasting room to try award-winning Bordeaux, Burgundian, and Rhone-styled wines. The shop has a great selection of wine-relevant gifts.

Wine lovers will have plenty to enjoy in Fredericksburg, as there are now nine wineries in Gillespie County and another five within easy driving distance. You'll find two custom wineries on Main Street (you create and bottle your own), as well as four wine tasting rooms, plus two wine bars downtown. For a map that lets you explore the wine options close to town, visit www.wineroad290 .com.

In Fredericksburg where US 290 becomes **Main Street,** you'll take in a wealth of vintage 1800s native limestone homes and commercial buildings, constructed in the German stone-and-mortar *fachwerk* fashion. The old structures form a corridor along Main, where dining, drinking, and browsing could occupy several weekends of your life. It's a good idea to drive up and down the street a few times to familiarize yourself with some storefronts, then tackle the span on foot. Pick up walking and driving maps at the **Fredericksburg Visitor Information Office,** 302 East Austin St. (888-997-3600 or 830-997-6523; www.visitfredericksburgTX.org). At the visitor center, find a theater showing a welcome DVD, free Internet access, and a large public restroom, along with a large, free parking lot.

Shopping is not a practice but an indulgent lifestyle in Fredericksburg. Browse the balance of the day away along Main in boutiques, shops, and stores that sell English and European antiques, American and Texan primitives, ranch-style table settings, old and new books, casual clothing, handmade candles, pewter beer steins, quilts, paintings, herbal remedies, and homegrown preserves and condiments.

DINNER Navajo Grill, 803 East Main St.; (830) 990-8289; www .navajogrill.com. One of Fredericksburg's fine dining spots, this is a destination for Southern cuisine given Southwestern and Creole influences. Specialties include cedar-planked salmon, skillet-roasted game hen, and penne pasta with shiitakes and pecan pesto. An excellent wine list is offered, too.

LODGING Choose from among 350 or so Fredericksburg-area B&Bs and guesthouses. Only about 25 percent of these are traditional B&Bs; many are houses or cottages you'll have all to yourself. The CVB offers a searchable database that you can browse according to price, location, amenities, number of guests with you, and so forth. There are pioneer log cabins, authentic *fachwerk* Sunday houses, rock buildings on Main Street, and rambling Victorian homes, along with ranches, farmhouses, and cabins out in the countryside.

DAY 2/MORNING

BREAKFAST At your B&B. If your craving for pastries has not been satisfied, **Rather Sweet Bakery,** 249 East Main St. (830-990-0498; www.rathersweet .com), serves some of the best food in town. Specialties include applewood-smoked bacon-cheddar scones; lemon-lime tarts; *kolaches;* sausage-cheese omelets, buttermilk pancakes, French toast, and oatmeal. Another good choice is **Fredericksburg Bakery,** 141 East Main St.; (830) 997-3254.

Start the day with a tour of the **National Museum of the Pacific War** 311 East Austin St. (830-997-8600; www.pacificwarmuseum .org). At the heart of the complex is an old hotel building that now houses exhibits on Admiral Chester W. Nimitz, who was born in Fredericksburg in 1885 and went on to become a five-star admiral, present at the signing of the Instrument of Surrender that marked the end of the war with Japan on September 2, 1945. Also at the museum, the vastly expanded **George H. W. Bush Gallery**, unveiled on Pearl Harbor Day, 2009, cost $15.3 million to improve.

At the hotel's back is the **Garden of Peace,** a lovely Oriental garden donated by the military leaders of Japan. Adjacent you'll find the **Memorial Wall,** which honors all who served and died in the war. The four-acre **History Walk of the Pacific,** a block east of the garden, includes relics such as planes, tanks, boats, and guns used in battles from Pearl Harbor to Tokyo Bay. See also **Plaza of the Presidents,** which recognizes ten U.S. presidents from Franklin Roosevelt to George H. W. Bush with service in World War II.

Continue west on Main a few blocks to the **Pioneer Museum Complex,** 325 West Main St. (830-997-2835), operated by the Gillespie County Historical Society. The museum's central building is the 1849 Kammlah House, which bears the Texas Historical Commission and National Historic Trust site markers. Tour eight furnished rooms, a wine cellar, a stone-floored yard, pioneer kitchens, a barn and smokehouse, a blacksmith shop, the Old First Methodist Church (1855), and a period log cabin. You'll also find a typical Sunday house, a unique Fredericksburg feature. These smallish, one-room homes with sleeping lofts were used by farmers and ranchers who would come to town to market on Saturday and stay for church on Sunday.

LUNCH   **Hondo's on Main,** 312 West Main St., Fredericksburg; (830) 997-1633 or (830) 997-1853; www.hondosonmain.com. Hondo's occupies a cool old native rock building and has one of the best patios in town. Be sure to go hungry, as the menu offers plenty in the way of filling, good food. Choose between mesquite-grilled burgers, spice-rubbed steak, barbecued pork ribs, Frito pie, stacked green chile-chicken enchiladas, crawfish sandwiches, giant salads—and plenty of grazing food if you just want to sip beer and snack the afternoon away.

AFTERNOON

Six blocks south of Main on Milam, you'll find **Fredericksburg Herb Farm,** 405 Whitney (830-997-8615; www.fredericksburgherbfarm .com). This exquisite herb garden, now undergoing an impressive expansion, is tended and harvested for the gourmet vinegars, teas, olive oils, seasonings, household potpourris, wreaths, bath potions, and fragrances that are sold here. A restaurant, shop, spa, and a selection of freestanding Sunday houses providing overnight stays are on-site.

Keep exploring the area's wine country. You can investigate the regional wineries with the help of maps provided by the **Texas Wine Trail** (www.texaswinetrail.com), which detail all two dozen of the Hill Country wineries. There are a number of weekend-long events offered on the wine trail throughout the year. Alternatively, with **Texas Wine Tours** (877-TEX-WINE; www.texas-wine-tours.com) you leave the driving to them—just go and enjoy half- and full-day winery tours that depart from Fredericksburg.

Also in this neck of the grapevines, visit **Wildseed Farms,** 7 miles east of Fredericksburg on US 290; (830-990-8080 or 800-848-0078; www.wildseedfarms.com). This giant producer of wildflower seeds—the outfit harvests about 400,000 pounds per year—provides hundreds of acres of explosive color for much of the year. At the farm center, visitors can see planting, harvesting, and flowers in varied growth stages. The market complex sells fresh-cut flowers, dried flowers, herbs, and hundreds of gifts that pertain to these goods. New to the compound are a beer garden, restaurant, and butterfly garden.

For something more offbeat visit **Luckenbach,** reached by driving 5 miles east of Fredericksburg on US 290, then south on RR 1376 about 4 miles. Made famous by the Willie Nelson–Waylon Jennings song, in which the crooners said, "In Luckenbach, Texas, ain't nobody feelin' no pain," the town of about twenty-five fun-lovin' folks has been called the Brigadoon of Texas. It mostly consists of a little post office, general store, tiny saloon, barbecue shack, and dance hall. There's often a Saturday night concert and dance and frequent music jams. For details call the general store at (830) 997-3224; www.luckenbachtexas.com.

DINNER   **August E's,** 203 East San Antonio, Fredericksburg; (830) 997-1585; www.august-es.com. New Zealand rack of lamb with balsamic-cherry glaze, mesquite-grilled steak, and shrimp scampi linguine are among the popular picks at this upscale dining spot, which also features a good wine list.

LODGING   At your B&B.

EVENING

Visit the **Rockbox Theater,** 109 North Llano St. (www.rockboxtheater
.com), for a selection of live musical and comedy shows each weekend. The show changes weekly, offering a variety of '50s, '60s, and
'70s music.

DAY 3/MORNING

BREAKFAST   At your B&B.

Head for **Enchanted Rock State Natural Area,** 18 miles north of Fredericksburg on RR 965 (325-247-3903). The centerpiece of the
1,643-acre spread is a billion-year-old pink granite monolith called
Enchanted Rock. The massive rock can be seen from miles away
but can be truly appreciated up close. In good weather, you might
find a crowd and a parking problem—so go early. Allow an hour to
climb to the top (wear good hiking or tennis shoes), then revel in
the views. Park rangers have excellent materials that describe the
geological and archaeological significance of the area.

Time to catch your flight home from Austin.

There's More . . . .

Blanco State Park, US 281 in Blanco; (830) 833-4333. The
lovely, spring-fed Blanco River passes beneath limestone hills of
the Edwards Plateau and flows through this charming, very old,
and very small state park to offer stressed-out travelers a respite
from all worries. One of the fifty-six New Deal parks built in Texas

by the Civilian Conservation Corps, the park was built in 1933–34. Find several old limestone buildings in a setting of oak, cypress, and cedar. Camping, hiking, picnicking, horseshoes, volleyball, and wildlife-watching are available.

Lady Bird Johnson Municipal Park, TX 16, 3 miles south of Fredericksburg; (830) 997-4202. The 190-acre park on Live Oak Creek has the new Live Oak Wilderness Trail, as well as woodsy picnic grounds with barbecue grills, a swimming pool, baseball diamonds, and volleyball and tennis courts. The twenty-acre lake is for fishing. Also at the park is the eighteen-hole Lady Bird Johnson Golf Course, open daily from 7 a.m. until dark and from noon on Mon. Call (830) 997-4010 for tee times.

Pedernales Falls State Park, 9 miles east of Johnson City via FR 2766; (830) 868-7304. An absolutely magnificent place to get in touch with nature and your own sense of peace, this park was formerly a ranch. The park's showpiece is a set of falls, where the Pedernales River drops some 50 feet over a 3,000-foot stretch, tumbling down slanting steps of layered limestone that is part of the 300-million-year-old Marble Falls formation of the Llano uplift. The park is dense with oak, juniper, pecan, elm, sycamore, walnut, and other trees, which provide a lovely home for white-tailed deer, coyotes, rabbits, armadillos, skunks, possums, raccoons, and more than 150 species of birds, including hawks, buzzards, herons, quail, doves, owls, roadrunners, wild turkeys, and the endangered golden-cheeked warbler. Hikers love the park, as do mountain bikers, horseback riders, campers, and picnickers.

Vereins Kirche Museum, Main at Crockett, Fredericksburg; (830) 997-2835. The landmark building is an eight-sided structure that replicates the original 1847 building, which was the town's church, school, meetinghouse, and fort for fifty years. Historical exhibits and archaeological finds are inside.

Special Events & Festivals . . . .

JUNE
Stonewall Peach Jamboree, Stonewall; www.stonewalltexas.com. Three days of frivolity includes a rodeo, queen's coronation, armadillo races, peach-eating and peach-pit-spitting contests and more.

JULY
Night in Old Fredericksburg; (866) 839-3378; www.tex-fest.com /niof/index.htm. Enjoy German and Texas music both days on two stages, arts and crafts, kids' area, and historic exhibits. Live music includes polka bands and country bands.

AUGUST
Gillespie County Fair, Fredericksburg; (830) 997-2359; www.gilles piefair.com. A parade kicks off the fun, which includes agricultural, livestock and home skills displays. Includes horse racing, concerts, dances, carnival and midway.

OCTOBER
Fredericksburg Food & Wine Fest, Fredericksburg; (830) 997-8515; www.fbgfoodandwinefest.com. More than 20 Texas wineries and a dozen chefs are showcased. There are food and wine pairing events, Gargantuan Great Grape Toss, auction, art, entertainment, and more.

Oktoberfest, Fredericksburg; (830) 997-4810; www.oktoberfest infbg.com. In the Marktplatz on West Main Street, find plenty of oompah in bratwurst, cold beer, a parade and opening ceremony, German, Czech, and Dutch music, a tuba jam, chicken dance block party, polka bands, food, a kinderpark, arts and crafts, clogging and much more.

DECEMBER
Candlelight Tour of Homes, Fredericksburg; (830) 997-2835; www .pioneermuseum.com. The Gillespie County Historical offers a Saturday-evening tour of historic houses decorated in period decor. Carolers sing, volunteers serve wine and traditional German cookies. There's a daytime tour, as well.

Other Recommended Restaurants & Lodgings . . . . .

FREDERICKSBURG
Auslander Biergarten, 323 East Main St.; (830) 997-7714. Greek salads, schnitzel, wurst, hot spiced wine, burgers.

Cabernet Grill at the Cotton Gin Village, just south of Fredericksburg on TX 16, (830) 990-5734, www.cabernetgrill.com. Steaks are the specialty here, and the restaurant claims to offer the largest Texas-only wine list in the state.

Cotton Gin Village, TX 16 South; (830) 990-8381; www.cottongin lodging.com. Rustic but posh cabins bring romance and comfort together.

Fredericksburg Bed & Brew, 245 East Main St.; (830) 997-6211; www.yourbrewery.com. Microbrewery and restaurant with a B&B upstairs.

Palo Alto Creek Farm, 90 Palo Alto Lane; (800) 997-0088; www
.paloaltocreekfarm.com. Pioneer homestead with two guesthouses,
whirlpools for two, and fireplaces.

Peach Tree Tea Room, 210 South Adams St.; (830) 997-9527;
www.peach-tree.com. Features include shrimp linguine, chicken
quesadillas, vegetable plates, quiche, and vanilla cheesecake with
praline sauce.

LUCKENBACH

The Full Moon Inn, Old Luckenbach Rd.; (830) 997-2205; www
.luckenbachtx.com. Restored 1860s log cabin with large fireplace,
full kitchen, private bath, full country breakfast.

For More Information . . . .

Fredericksburg Convention and Visitors Bureau, 106 North Adams
St., Fredericksburg, TX 78624; (830) 997-6523; www.fredericks
burg-texas.com.

Johnson City Chamber of Commerce, 404 West Main St., P.O. Box
485, Johnson City, TX 78636; (830) 868-7684; www.lbjcountry
.com.

SOUTHBOUND ESCAPE *Ten*

South Padre Island and the Rio Grande Valley (By Plane)

THE BEACH AND THE BAY/2 NIGHTS

Beachfront condos
Bodysurfing
Fishing
Jet Skiing
Horseback riding
Sailing
Seafood
Wildlife
Tropical produce
Historic sites

At Texas's southernmost point, the barrier island just off the mainland is the vaunted South Padre Island. An especially skinny finger of sand, this 34-mile-long section was separated from the upper 92-mile reach when the Port Mansfield cut was opened in 1964. For years there were just a couple of motel resorts and vacation houses that looked out at the Gulf of Mexico, and now and then people from Dallas/Fort Worth and other quarters of the state would make long, arduous drives through south Texas to walk along the dunes, fish, and bake in the sun.

The development-crazed 1970s and 1980s changed the tempo of South Padre considerably, however, and today, many travelers say this beach destination—which offers more than 7,000 hotel and condo rooms—rivals more exalted sandy spots in Florida, the Carolinas, and even Mexico. Note that during spring breaks, from late Feb until mid-Apr, the island is jamming with some 100,000 high school and college students who come to party in a big way from all over the United States and Canada. The rest of the year, Winter Texans or "snowbirds" from the upper states—and real Texans, of course—find South Padre a very pleasant getaway, with an abundance of restaurants, shopping centers, nightclubs, and high-rise hotels and condos. Airports in Harlingen and Brownsville

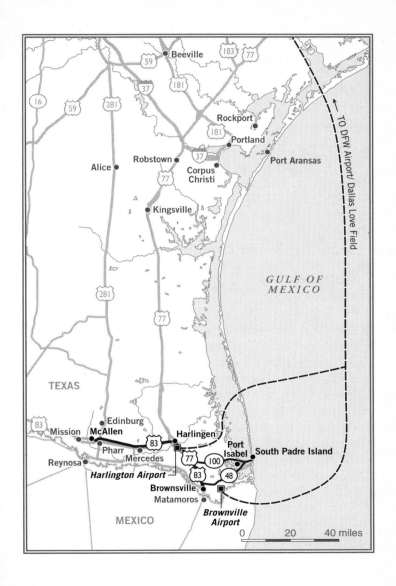

are less than an hour's drive to the beach. There's something to do on or next to the water every hour of the day. The only difficulty encountered on this escape lies in deciding whether to do everything or nothing at all.

DAY 1/MORNING

The only quick way to go to South Padre Island from North Texas is to catch an hour-long flight from either DFW Airport or Dallas Love Field to Harlingen, a forty-five-minute drive from South Padre, or Brownsville, a twenty-five-minute drive from the island. When you land, take a rental car to the beach; rental agencies provide maps for the easy drive.

Just before you reach the island, stop in the vintage fishing village of Port Isabel to stock up on provisions, which are more expensive in island grocery stores. Several fish markets that line the main road sell huge, fresh shrimp and myriad fresh fish fillets. Before you drive across the causeway to the island, stop at **Port Isabel Lighthouse State Historic Park,** TX 100 and Tarvana Street at the Causeway (421 E. Queen Isabella Blvd.; 956-943-1172; www .tpwd.state.tx.us). The smallest state park and the only lighthouse on the coast open to the public, the beacon here shone 16 miles into the Gulf from its opening in 1853 until its closing in 1905. If you've got the leg power, climb the winding seventy-plus steps to the top to gain a great view of Port Isabel, the Causeway, South Padre Island, and the Gulf of Mexico beyond.

Now cross the blue Laguna Madre Bay on the Queen Isabella Causeway, Texas's longest bridge, stretching a little more than 2½ miles. The center span rises 73 feet above the mean high tide, which allows ships heading to sea to pass below. Its strength will withstand threefold hurricane-force winds. At the causeway's end, you're greeted by the statue of Padre Nicolas Balli, the first European said to have settled here.

At the foot of the bridge lies the city of South Padre Island, where all island development is concentrated. The visitor center is right there at 600 Padre Blvd. (956-761-6433 or 800-767-2373; www.sopadre.com). Now check into your condo and kick back.

LODGING There are three condo rooms for every hotel or motel room on the island, and these are usually very nice vacation homes. Having your own kitchen saves cash, too. The South Padre Island Convention and Visitors Bureau and local reservation agencies (both listed at end of chapter) can provide dozens of ideas for the more than one hundred choices in lodging establishments. Some of the more popular choices are **Sunchase IV** (800-944-6818), **Suntide III** (800-847-5728; www.suntideiii.com), **Bridgepoint** (800-221-1402; www.bridgepointresort.com), and **Bahia Mar** (800-997-2373). Hotel chains include **Days Inn, Super 8, Holiday Inn, Radisson,** and **Sheraton.**

LUNCH In your condo; fresh shrimp is the most likely idea, and it's never better than here. Or try **Amberjack's Bayside Bar & Grill,** 209 West Amberjack; (956) 761-6500; www.amberjacks-spi.com. A wonderful view of the bay goes well with fresh fish, steaks, pasta, burgers, and salads.

AFTERNOON

Enjoy the beach. There are childlike joys found in just jumping in to ride the waves. As you roam the sand, you're likely to encounter Sandy Feet, a legendary architect of sand-castle creations. You could also easily wander into a volleyball game, too. Specific beach destinations include **Andy Bowie Park,** 4 miles north of town (956-761-3704). There are picnic pavilions and a children's playground here, and this is also where you'll find the **Island Equestrian Center**

(956-761-4677; www.horsesonthebeach.com), with horse and pony rides on the beach daily, as well as guides and instruction.

At the opposite end of the beach, south almost as far as you can drive, there's **Isla Blanca Park** (956-761-5493), with RV camping, two picnic pavilions, jetty fishing, and good eating at **Sea Ranch Marina.** Fun for the kids is at **Jeremiah's** (956-761-2131), where waterslides, miniature golf, a driving range, a video arcade, and sand-castle-building instruction are offered. Isla Blanca is also home to the **University of Texas–Pan American Coastal Studies Laboratory** (956-761-2644), with its aquarium and extensive shell collection.

If you like packaged fun on the sand, head to **Schlitterbahn,** 90 Park Rd., South Padre Island (956-772-7873 or 956-772-9772; www.schlitterbahn.com). This full-blown water park overlooking the Gulf has it all: Hop on Rio Aventura, a never-ending river linking each attraction and float to Rio Beach and its massive wave lagoon, ride the rapids and currents through chutes or to beaches. Families have **Sandcastle Cove,** with shallow play pools and an interactive sand castle, and surfers can hang ten at the **Boogie Bahn,** with the nation's biggest man-made surfing wave.

Anglers have plenty of options available. Half- and full-day fishing trips in the Laguna Madre Bay and the Gulf of Mexico range in cost from $14 to $1,000, depending on what you're after. Talk to fishing charter captains—who will help you catch whiting, drum, flounder, trout, redfish, kingfish, wahoo, tuna, marlin, and sailfish—about specific trips. Contact **Jim's Pier** (956-761-2865), **Fisherman's Wharf** (956-761-7818; 800-752-9889), or the **Sea Ranch Marina** (956-761-7777; www.searanchmarina.net).

Anything you could possibly need and didn't bring—from a new swimsuit, hat, sunblock, radio, or piece of jewelry to pizza, beer, video rentals, or bicycles—is available in stores that line about a 30-block reach of Padre Boulevard. If you never see movies at home, there's a cinema here.

DINNER Either grill fish and steaks at your condo, or head to **Black-beard's,** 103 East Saturn (956-761-2962; www.blackbeardsspi.com), for outstanding blackened shrimp fajitas, other seafood, and steaks.

LODGING At your condo or hotel.

DAY 2/MORNING

BREAKFAST At your condo or hotel.

Consider a visit to **Sea Turtle, Inc.,** a research and education facility dedicated to the preservation of Kemp's ridley sea turtles and seven other endangered species of marine turtles. Your $3 donation is a real bargain. Tours usually start at 10 a.m. and run for half an hour Tues through Sun at 6617 Padre Blvd. They run continuously until 3: 30 p.m. Call (956) 761-4511 or visit www.seaturtleinc.com for information.

For a solitary beach day, take a drive south to Brazos Island. To get there, head back across the causeway to TX 48 South to TX 511 and go south to TX 4; you'll then go east on Texas 4 to **Boca Chica,** the main beach on Brazos Island, where the road runs out. Few people wander down to these white sands; bring a picnic.

There's a historical marker on TX 4 that notes the site of the last Civil War battle. Interestingly, it was fought near here on May 12–13, 1865, more than a month after Lee surrendered at Appomattox, and the Union troops had been forced back into their fort on Brazos Island when they received word of the Confederate surrender.

LUNCH Picnic on the beach.

AFTERNOON

While away the afternoon on the beach or make a trip to **Laguna Atascosa National Wildlife Refuge,** a twenty-minute drive north of Port Isabel at FR 106 and FR 1847 (956-748-3608; www.fws .gov/refuges). The 46,000-acre preserve is the marshland, freshwater, and saltwater home to thousands of orioles, bluebirds, Harris's hawks, and kiskadee flycatchers, among others. Other residents include coyote, bobcat, javelina, and deer. Tours are taken by car or on foot, and the visitor center contains wildlife exhibits. The park is open daily sunup to sunset, and the visitor center is open 10 a.m. to 4 p.m. daily Oct through Apr and weekends only in May. There is a $3 charge per vehicle.

If you prefer a bit of history, head just about a half hour from the beach via TX 48 to Brownsville, where the Mexican-American War was ignited. Two important battlefields are near town: **Palo Alto Battlefield,** north at FR 1847 and FR 511, and **Resaca de la Palma Battlefield,** on FR 1847 between Price and Coffeeport Streets.

Far more peaceful is **Brownsville's Gladys Porter Zoo,** 500 Ringgold at 6th Street (956-546-7187; www.gpz.org). Considered by experts as one of the top ten zoos in the nation, this one is special since it has no bars or cages to contain animals but rather moats and waterways. Around 1,800 birds, mammals, and reptiles represent five continents, and a children's zoo lets kids pet little critters.

DINNER   Watch boats coming in at sunset at **Sea Ranch Restaurant,** 1 Padre Blvd.; (956) 761-1314; www.searanchrestaurant.com. Start with peel-and-eat shrimp or oysters Rockefeller, then spoil yourself with grilled, freshly caught red snapper or blackened scallops. Not into fish? Try a rib eye or pasta dish. Or enjoy a seat right next to **Laguna Madre at Louie's Backyard,** 2305 Laguna Blvd.; (956) 761-6406; www.lbyspi.com. There's a seafood and prime rib buffet every evening.

NIGHTLIFE　　No longer a sleepy town, South Padre specializes in dance clubs and watering holes. Some of the favorite spots, in addition to Louie's (aforementioned), include **Chaos,** 1601 Padre Blvd. (www.spichaos.com), with six clubs under one roof; **Kelly's Irish Pub,** at 101 East Morningside Dr. (956-433-5380); **Coral Reef,** with piano bar and pool tables, at 5401 Padre Blvd. (956-761-1813); and **Tequila Sunset,** with live music and more than forty premium tequilas, at 200 West Pike (956-761-6198; www.tequilasunset.com).

LODGING　　Your condo.

DAY 3/MORNING

BREAKFAST　　Make breakfast in your condo.

Spend your last seaside morning enjoying the island wildlife. Book a tour with **Colley's Fins to Feathers** (956-299-0629; www .fin2feather.com), which departs the Sea Ranch Marina on South Padre Island, near Isla Blanca Park. Scarlett and George Colley have cultivated a careful, respectful relationship with several families of dolphins living in the Laguna Madre, and they'll take you to visit their entertaining pals and share stories of their intriguing adventures. The Colleys are well-versed birders, too, and can customize your tour to include waterfowl.

LUNCH　　On your way toward the airport, stop in Port Isabel for a quick but terrific lunch at one of two great finds. At **Isabel's Cafe,** TX 100 at Port Road (956-943-5082), stupendous, chubby soft tacos and burritos keep the masses happy. Hungry-man fish plates are served at **Fisherman's,** 416 Hwy. 100; (956) 943-4545.

AFTERNOON

Head to the Harlingen or Brownsville airport, where you'll catch a flight home.

There's More . . . .

Golf. Among several other good courses, two choices are **Treasure Hills Country Club,** 3017 Treasure Hills in Harlingen (956-365-3100 or 956-425-1700; www.treasurehillsgc.com), a Robert Trent Jones–designed, eighteen-hole course; and **Rancho Viejo Country Club,** just west of US 77/83, 3 miles north of Brownsville (956-350-4000, 956-350-5696 or 800-531-7400; www.playrancho.com), which offers two eighteen-hole, par 70 championship courses.

Sailboarding. From Sept through May, sailboarders will be challenged by daytime winds that average 18 mph in the bay and at the Jetties, Boca Chica, and the Ditch. For conditions, equipment, and rentals, contact **Windsurf Inc.** on the Bay (956-761-1434 or 800-880-5423; www.windsurfinc.com) or **Windsurf the Boatyard** (956-761-5061; www.windsurftheboatyard.com).

Special Events & Festivals . . . .

LATE JULY

Texas International Fishing Tournament; (956) 943-8438; www.tift .org. The weekend includes a family play day with games, contests and prizes for kids; two full days of competitive fishing for game fish; and a fish fry with awards presentation.

MID-OCTOBER

Sand Castle Days, South Padre Island. Professional sandcastle masters build elaborate palaces in high-stakes competition, while families compete in amateur divisions; (956) 761-6433; www .sandcastledays.com.

Other Recommended Restaurants & Lodgings . . . . .

The Brown Pelican Inn, 207 West Aries, South Padre Island; (956) 761-2722; www.brownpelican.com. Eight guest rooms furnished with European and American antiques; private baths, covered porches, and a Laguna Madre view make this a nice alternative to condos.

Palm Street Pier Bar and Grill, 204 West Palm St., South Padre Island; (956) 772-7256; www.palmstreetpier.com. Locals and visitors alike flock to this laid-back place with the great bay view. Shrimp dishes abound.

Sheraton Fiesta Beachside Grill in Sheraton Beach Resort, 310 Padre Blvd., South Padre Island; (956) 761-6551. Breakfast, lunch, and dinner are accompanied by a Gulf view.

For More Information . . . .

South Padre Island Convention and Visitors Bureau, 600 Padre Blvd., South Padre Island, TX 78597; (956) 761-6433 or (800) 767-2373; www.sopadre.com.

Condominium reservation agencies include **Padre Island Rentals** (800-926-6926; www.superpadre.net) and **AACE Condo Rentals** (800-828-2223; www.aace-rent.com).

NORTHBOUND ESCAPES

NORTHBOUND ESCAPE *One*

Lake Texoma, Lake Murray, and Turner Falls (By Car)

CROSSING THE RED RIVER/2 NIGHTS

Fishing
Sailing
Waterskiing
History
Houseboating
Golf and tennis
Horseback riding
Children's programs
Cabins
Camping
Catfish
Cookies

Leaving concrete, expressways, and prairie behind, escapists looking for some watery adventures can find them on the Red River. Driving less than ninety minutes, travelers from the Metroplex find loads of recreation at massive Lake Texoma, created by damming the historic river that acts as a boundary between Texas and Oklahoma. Retreat to a lovely resort, a simple fishing cabin, or a houseboat.

Smaller and a bit more remote, Lake Murray is a woodsy sanctuary, also rich in recreation possibilities. North Texans who haven't ventured this way are amazed at Lake Murray's pretty setting and depth of offerings.

Indeed across the Red River in Oklahoma await many pleasant, outdoorsy surprises near the lakes, primarily in the form of a low granite range called the Arbuckle Mountains. Scientists have termed the area one of three geological windows into the past, placing it in league with the Grand Canyon of Arizona and the Black Hills of South Dakota.

Scattered around the 300-million-year-old uplift are an abundance of trees, streams, and lakes that defy the Sooner State's prairie–Dust Bowl image.

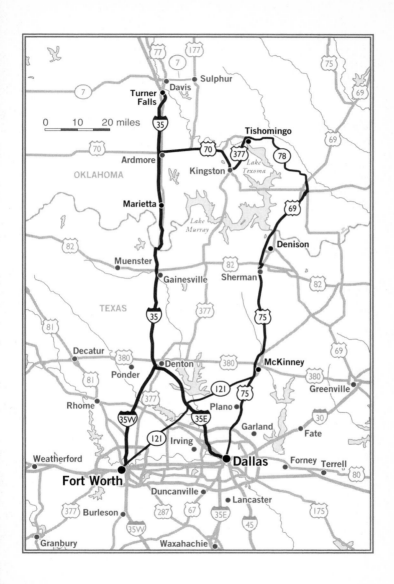

DAY 1/MORNING

From Dallas, the drive to Lake Texoma is an easy 75 miles north on US 75. From Fort Worth take TX 121 North to McKinney and pick up US 75 there.

BREAKFAST Slow down and enjoy a country breakfast at the old-fashioned **Bill Smith's Cafe,** 1500 West University Dr. in McKinney; (972) 542-5331.

If you're taking your time heading to the lakes, look around McKinney for a bit. There are dozens of shops in restored buildings around the square that offer antiques, art, and gift items. Several buildings downtown and in nearby **Chestnut Square** tell the town's story, which began when settlers arrived in 1841 from Kentucky, Arkansas, and Tennessee. The town, which became the seat of Collin County in 1848, was home to James W. Throckmorton, the eleventh governor of Texas, who later served in the U.S. Congress. McKinney also played host to Jesse and Frank James when the James Gang came to visit their cousin "Tuck" Hill, whose historic house still stands just west of downtown at 616 West Virginia St.

Continue north on US 75 to Denison and the **Eisenhower birthplace,** 208 East Day St., Visitor's Center at 609 S. Lamar Ave. (903-465-8908; www.visiteisenhowerbirthplace.com). The five-star general and two-term U.S. president, Dwight D. Eisenhower, is honored at the home where he was born on October 14, 1890. Although he moved with his family soon afterward to Abilene, Kansas, the site is a popular one for Texans. A large bronze statue of Ike stands in front of the simple cottage, and guided walks on the ten-acre reserve are offered.

Leave US 75 and take FR 120 northwest to Pottsboro and the south shore of **Lake Texoma Recreation Area,** a U.S. Army Corps of Engineers creation that covers 193,859 acres in two states. The

89,000-acre lake—impounded by Denison Dam—is held in highest regard by anglers in search of striper and myriad other bass. Marinas are numerous, with offerings that range from guided fishing charters to pontoon boat rentals, waterskiing, sailing, Jet Skiing, yachting, and houseboating. For information phone the U.S. Army Corps of Engineers at (903) 465-4990. Enjoy the drive, as the smaller roads cut through pretty, wooded stretches populated mostly by longhorn and cutting horse ranches.

Highport Marina, 120 Texoma Harbor Dr. in Pottsboro (903-786-7000 or 800-569-4650; www.highport.com), is a good place to hook up with fishing guides and boat charters/rentals.

LUNCH   **Huck's Catfish,** 2811 S. Trail Dr. in Denison; (903) 337-0033. Farm-raised fish are served inside this pretty brick building fashioned in the style of a farmhouse with a big front porch.

AFTERNOON

Not fishing, skiing, sailing, or swimming? Then spend the rest of the day on the golf course or tennis courts at Tanglewood Resort Hotel (see Lodging below).

If houseboating sounds like a better idea, head over to the lake's northeast shore by driving north from Denison on US 75 into Oklahoma, continuing north to the Durant area, where you'll take US 70 west a short distance to **Willow Springs Resort and Marina,** near Mead (580-924-6240 or 888-468-6240). Heated, air-conditioned houseboats range from 40 feet to 56 feet and sleep from two to fourteen people; they're available for weekends or by the week and come with kitchens and baths.

DINNER   Either cook out on the houseboat grill or stay in Pottsboro and dine at **Tanglewood Resort** on steak, trout, pasta, or chicken.

LODGING   **Tanglewood Resort Hotel,** 290 Tanglewood Circle, Pottsboro; (903) 786-2968 or (800) 833-6569; www.tanglewoodresort.com. On Lake Texoma's southern shore, this resort has four swimming pools, a hot tub, an eighteen-hole golf course, ski boat and Wave Runner rentals, horseback riding, volleyball, horseshoes, croquet, and guided fishing trips. There are a little more than 300 hotel and condo rooms and suites.

DAY 2/MORNING

BREAKFAST   Feast on waffles and bacon at Tanglewood Resort before heading to the Oklahoma side of the lake. Go north from Denison on US 75 to Durant, picking up US 70 west to Kingston, then follow US 377 north to Tishomingo.

At the northern end of Lake Texoma, the town of Tishomingo serves as the capital of the Chickasaw Nation. To gain some insight into this historic culture, visit the **Chickasaw Bank Museum** and **Johnston County Museum of History,** 100 South Capital in Tishomingo; (580) 371-0254. This restored building was the Chickasaw tribe's bank at the turn of the 20th century. Visit it Mon through Fri. Then see the **Chickasaw Council House Museum,** 209 North Fisher Ave.; (580) 371-3351. The Chickasaw's history, from the Trail of Tears removal through the modern day, is detailed. There's a genealogy center and a small retail shop, too.

Head now to Lake Murray, driving west from Madill on US 70, then into Oklahoma via OK 77 South.

LUNCH   **Lake Murray Lodge** (see Lodging below). **The Apple Bin Restaurant** offers sandwiches, plate lunches, soups, salads, and desserts.

AFTERNOON

Only about a half-hour's drive west of Lake Texoma, the forested playground of 12,496-acre **Lake Murray State Park** (580-223-4044; www.oklahomaparks.com) awaits you. Wrapping around a 5,700-acre lake, the park offers golfing on an eighteen-hole course, horseback riding, fishing, waterskiing, tennis, hiking, bike riding, canoeing, and nature study. Check the bulletin boards to see what outdoor programs and water games are offered for children each day.

DINNER   **Fireside Dining,** adjacent to Lake Murray resort park; (580) 226-4070. Cozy spot serves steaks, chicken, fish, salads, and pasta.

LODGING   **Lake Murray Lodge,** 2 miles directly east of I-35 and exit 24; (580) 223-6600; (800) 257-0322. There are fifty-two guest rooms and suites, as well as eighty-one cottages, some with fireplaces and kitchenettes. Or, book a room out in the countryside about fifteen minutes northeast of Ardmore at the **Shiloh Morning Inn,** off Oklahoma 199; (888) 554-7674; (580) 223-9500; www.shiloh morning.com. Built specifically as an inn on seventy-three acres, this charming retreat has five large suites with big whirlpool tubs and ample sitting areas, cable TV, phone, and privacy. Two separate cottages offer utter escape with kitchenettes, hot tubs on screened-in porches, and plenty of woods in which to roam. From a professional-size kitchen comes huge breakfasts, including amazing baked goods, elaborate egg dishes, and fruit smoothies.

DAY 3/MORNING

Rise early and take a long bike ride or hike—or sleep in (this is a vacation, for heaven's sake). Or make plans to play golf at the Lake Murray resort's eighteen-hole course; (580) 223-6613. Either way, plan on a late breakfast.

BREAKFAST   At the Lake Murray Lodge coffee shop. Make this brunch by filling up on ham and eggs, hash browns, and biscuits and gravy.

Explore one of the park's more unusual attractions, **Tucker Tower,** a grand structure in a beautiful setting perched high above the lakeshore that looks much like a castle or fortress. Begun in 1933, it was intended to be the Oklahoma governor's retreat. Unfinished, it went unused until the state made it a museum in the 1950s. Some interesting exhibits include part of a gargantuan meteorite that crashed nearby, as well as fossils and wildlife exhibits. For information, phone (580) 223-2109. Call for hours.

Or, continue north on I-35 about thirty minutes, watching for the **Turner Falls** exit (51) at Davis, Oklahoma, when the highway's path begins to cut through huge humps of rock. From the exit follow OK 77 South about 2 miles to **Turner Falls Park** (580-369-2917 or 580-369-2988; www.turnerfallspark.com). Oklahoma's oldest park is a delight for naturalists. Numerous springs pour from the Arbuckles to form **Honey Creek,** and a cascade tumbles 77 feet into a natural pool that serves as Turner Falls Park's centerpiece.

Travelers searching for refreshing beauty have been visiting Turner Falls since 1868. Today the 720-acre park is operated by the city of Davis, and the falls are lighted at night. There are scenic picnic areas in the park; nature and hiking trails; intriguing rocks and other geological formations, such as Wagon Wheel Cave and Outlaw Cave; trout fishing in winter; volleyball courts; bathhouses; campsites; sandy beaches; and plenty of swimming. In the dog days of summer, this refreshing spot is unbeatable. Be aware that overcrowding on weekends is not unusual, so make a weekday visit when possible.

LUNCH   Pick up groceries in Davis for a picnic at Turner Falls.

Take another hike in Turner Falls or in the Chickasaw National Recreation Area. Then point your car south on I-35 again to head home.

There's More . . . .

Boggy Depot State Park, about 30 miles northeast of Tishomingo via Oklahoma Highways 99 and 7; (580) 889-5625. A six-acre lake with fishing is the centerpiece of this 630-acre park, which features nature trails, camping, and a playground.

Chickasaw National Recreation Area, (580) 622-3165; is 11 miles east of Turner Falls at the town of Sulphur on OK 177, and spreads across nearly 10,000 wooded acres and is ideal for nature lovers and families. Streams and little waterfalls populate the park, and springs here—imbued with sulphur and bromide—have long been enjoyed for their healing qualities. Lake of the Arbuckles, which covers 2,350 acres, is formed by Arbuckle Dam where Buckhorn, Guy Sandy, and Rock Creeks merge. Swimming, waterskiing, sailing, and bass fishing are popular on these waters, and six campgrounds are on-site. For Wave Runner, Jet Ski, and pontoon boat rentals, call **Arbuckle Boat Rentals** at (580) 622-5790; www.arbuckleboatrentals.com.

The park is home to a small herd of buffalo, descendants of the millions that roamed this territory a century ago. In summer, ranger-led programs include campfire talks and nature walks. Wildlife study, live animals, exhibits, and demonstrations are offered at the **Travertine Nature Center** (580-622-7234).

Hagerman National Wildlife Refuge, at the southern end of Big Mineral Arm on Lake Texoma, FR 1417 west of Denison; (903) 786-2826. This 11,320-acre preserve is the winter home for many ducks and geese and a feeding place for migratory birds. Fishing, hiking, picnicking, and a visitor center with wildlife exhibits are available.

Special Events & Festivals . . . .

APRIL
Ardmoredillo Chili Cookoff, Ardmore, Oklahoma; (580) 226-6246. Competition for best chili and showmanship, with children's rodeo clown costumes and plenty of music. Ardmore Chamber; (580) 223-7765.

Texoma Lakefest Regatta, Denison, Texas; www.texomalakefest .com. Texoma Sailing Club; (903) 337-0532; www.texomasailing .org. Denison Chamber; (903) 465-1551. A premiere sailing race is the main draw. The Regatta benefits Texas-area children's charities and was the first of its kind in the US.

JUNE
Sand Bass Festival, Madill, Oklahoma; www.sandbassfestival.com. Marshall County Chamber; (580) 795-2431. Arts and crafts, midway carnival, car show, fishing contests, fun run and nightly concerts fill a busy bill of events on the courthouse square.

LATE SEPTEMBER–EARLY OCTOBER
Chickasaw Festival, Tishomingo, Oklahoma; (580) 371-2040 and (800) 593-3356. Historical and cultural events mixed with a junior Olympics, craft and art market, and rodeo.

Other Recommended Restaurants & Lodgings . . . . .

ARDMORE, OKLAHOMA
Cattle Rustlers Steakhouse, 110 Holiday Dr.; (580) 223-7848; www.cattlerustlerssteakhouse.com. Prime rib, rib eyes, chicken, and fish dinners.

DAVIS, OKLAHOMA
Cabins at Cedarvale, OK 77 South near Turner Falls; (580) 369-3224; www.cedarvalegardens.com. Big, one-bedroom cabins with giant fireplaces, kitchenettes, outdoor grills, and picnic tables.

DENISON, TEXAS
The Molly Cherry Victorian Bed and Breakfast, 200 West Molly Cherry Lane; (903) 465-0575; www.mollycherry.com. An 1890 Queen Anne home on six acres in woods; lovely 9-foot-tall stained glass in entry doors.

MARIETTA, OKLAHOMA
McGehee's Catfish Restaurant, exit 15 off I-35 in Marietta; (580) 276-2751. If it's 1 p.m. or later on Saturday or Sunday, heading to this popular place for feasting on catfish has a devoted clientele; some even fly private planes up from Dallas/Fort Worth to a grassy landing strip nearby for dinner. The restaurant opens at 5 p.m. weekdays. Closed Wed.

POTTSBORO, TEXAS
Flowing Wells Resort, 3217 Flowing Wells Rd.; (903) 786-2930; www.flowingwellsresort.com. Cabins on a thirty-one-acre wooded lakefront with boat ramp and boat rentals.

Lighthouse Resort and Marina, 300 Lighthouse Dr., Pottsboro, Texas; (903) 786-2311; www.lighthouseresort.com. Thirty-four fully equipped cabins (some are trailers) with cable TV; restaurant; fishing charters and guides, bait and tackle, boat rentals; swimming beach; RV hookups, campground; boutique.

For More Information . . . .

Ardmore Chamber of Commerce, 410 West Main St., Ardmore, OK 73402; (580) 223-7765.

Davis Chamber of Commerce, 300 East Main St., Davis, OK 73030; (580) 369-2402.

Denison Chamber of Commerce, 313 West Woodard St., Denison, TX 75020; (903) 465-1551.

Oklahoma Parks and Resorts, (800) 652-6552; www.oklahoma parks.com.

Pottsboro Chamber of Commerce, (903) 786-6371; www.texoma lake.com.

Denton and Gainesville (By Car)
VICTORIANA, ANTIQUES, AND BARGAINS/1 NIGHT

F ew Dallas/Fort Worth residents seem to be familiar with Denton, though it's just a half hour north of the Metroplex. Those who do may have attended the University of North Texas or Texas

- Antiques shops
- German heritage and food
- Factory outlet malls
- Barbecue and steaks

Woman's University, both situated in the Denton County seat. Established in 1857, downtown Denton is rife today with architectural trophies from its early years.

Gainesville, also packed with beautiful old homes and buildings, is another historic town that peacefully rides the rolling north Texas plains, which are rich in quarter-horse ranches. It was founded in 1850. Gainesville's earliest visitors were 49ers headed to California during the Gold Rush, and some Gainesville ancestors were freethinkers in their day: Most Texans wanted secession in the 1860s, but some Cooke County folks who opposed it created a secret society supporting the Union.

DAY 1/MORNING

Drive north from Dallas on I-35E, or from Fort Worth on I-35W; the highways merge in Denton, barely 30 miles north of either city. Visit the information office at 414 West Parkway St. in town for maps, etc. (940-382-7895; www.discoverdenton.com).

BREAKFAST **The Chestnut Tree Tea Room,** 107 W. Hickory St., across from the Denton County Courthouse-on-the-Square; (940) 591-9475; www.chest

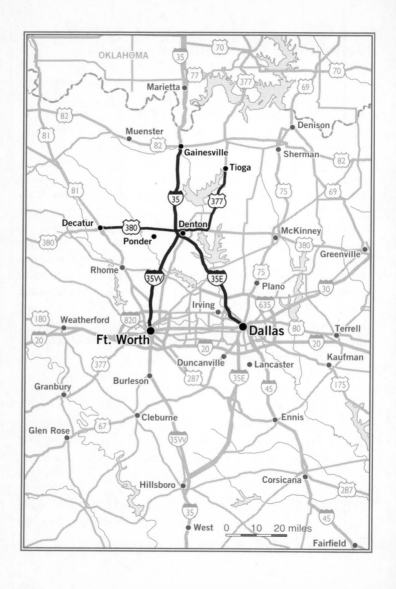

nuttearoom.com. Eggs Florentine, whole wheat pancakes and waffles, plus ham and cheese crepes, will give you plenty of fuel for the day.

Nearby find Denton's historic district laden with landmark sites; an excellent self-guided tour map for driving or walking is offered at the visitor center in town. Among several intriguing homes and buildings is **Little Chapel in the Woods**, at Bell and University Streets on Texas Woman's University campus. It was designed and built by noted architect O'Neil Ford in 1939; First Lady Eleanor Roosevelt attended the dedication ceremonies. Considered an outstanding structure, the chapel is an example of the marriage of art and nature. Stained-glass windows (designed by students) depict themes, "women ministering to human needs." **The Gowns of the First Ladies of Texas Exhibit,** housed in the TWU Administration Conference Tower (940-898-3644), is a fabulous display of the inaugural gowns (originals or faithful replicas) of the First Ladies of Texas. The collection also includes gowns of Mamie Eisenhower, Lady Bird Johnson, and Barbara Bush, worn during their husbands' terms in the White House.

See also the museum inside the **Denton County Courthouse,** 110 West Hickory St. on the square in Denton (940-349-2850; www.dentoncounty.com/chos). Built between 1895 and 1897 of limestone from a local quarry, gray sandstone from Mineral Wells, and red granite from Burnet County, the exquisite creation houses the Denton County Historical Museum on its first floor. Among several displays are a doll collection, a Victorian parlor, and a period country kitchen.

At the Denton Central Fire Station, the **Denton Firefighters' Museum,** 332 East Hickory St., (940-349-8840) near the square, honors firefighters from the past through the present. There are historic artifacts, a 1935 ladder truck, antique gear, and volumes of daily fire report logs.

A fabulous find for bibliophiles is **Recycled Books, Records & CDs,** on the northeast corner of the square at 200 North Locust St. (940-566-5688; www.recycledbooks.com). The three-story, 17,000-square-foot store stocks 200,000 books and more than 12,000 CDs and ships to customers around the world. It's known as a favorite of Texas's Pulitzer Prize–winning author Larry McMurtry, too.

Old and new goods are found at **Western Heritage Gallery,** 5800 North I-35; (214) 912-8896; www.thewesternheritagegallery.com. An ongoing show of western goods, this is a giant gallery that exhibits cowboy-cowgirl boots, chaps, saddles, and more, along with handcrafted furnishing and artwork that includes oils and bronzes.

You could easily devote a day to the **North Texas Horse Country Tour,** a self-guided route of farms where quarter horses, thoroughbreds, paints, Arabians, Appaloosas, and more are bred and trained. Find the farms outlined at www.horsecountrytours.com. The **Denton Convention and Visitors Bureau** also schedules behind-the-scenes tours; book your seat by calling (800) 381-1818 or visit www.discoverdenton.com.

LUNCH **Rudy's Country Store,** 520 South I-35 Frontage Rd., Denton; (940) 484-RUDY; www.rudys.com. This famous barbecue joint out of San Antonio will impress. You work your way through a serving line, picking out all the goodies you want, then sit at picnic tables in the barnlike restaurant and chow down. Sandwiches include smoked pork loin, beef brisket, and sausage; you can opt for a plate with smoked chicken or turkey, pork ribs, chopped beef, or sliced beef. It's a friendly place suited for young and old.

Go north and west a bit along country roads to Muenster for a rich, tasty cultural experience. **The Center Restaurant and Tavern,** right on US 82 (940-759-2910; www.thecenterrestaurant.com), sits in the middle of a minute town settled in 1889 and still thick with German heritage. A cheery and popular place, it's tops for Wiener schnitzel, German potato salad and sauerkraut, homemade sausages, excellent chicken noodle soup, and apple strudel.

AFTERNOON

From Denton it's a 30-mile drive north on I-35 to Gainesville. A most charming courthouse square is found just east of I-35 on California where it intersects Commerce and Dixon. More than two dozen 19th-century buildings crowd the square's brick streets. Seen easily on foot, some of the noteworthy sites (take a loaded camera) are the **James Hosapple Saloon,** built in 1885 on the north side of the square; the 1883 **First National Bank Building,** at the northeast corner of California and Dixon; and the 1915 **Cooke County Jail,** on Dixon between Pecan and Main. At the square's center is the **Cooke County Courthouse,** a 1910 monument.

Travelers who enjoy a good walk or drive may see more than thirty other remarkable homes and buildings in Gainesville. A visitor guide from the local chamber of commerce (see For More Information) details a route that leads south on Dixon from the square, east on Church, then both north and south on Denton. Structures include spectacular homes built between 1882 and 1927, churches from 1884 and 1912, and the 1902 Santa Fe Depot.

There are plenty of antiques haunts in Gainesville, mostly clustered around the square. Among Texans' favorite shopping stops are the **Gainesville Outlet Shops,** I-35 at exit 501 (940-668-6092; www.gainesvilleoutletshops.com). Some one hundred stores offer discounts of 25 to 75 percent off typical retail prices. Famous store names include Gap, Van Heusen, Reebok, Kitchen Collection, SAS Factory Store, Oshkosh B'Gosh, and Zales Outlet.

DINNER   **Clark's Outpost,** 101 Texas 377 at Gene Autry Lane in Tioga; (940) 437-2414. Reach tiny Tioga in this rolling horse-ranch country by traveling east from Denton on US 380 for 7 miles, then north on US 377 for 16 miles. Blink and you might miss the brown roadhouse that seems to lean a bit. Inside find warm, friendly dining rooms; neighborly service; and savory meals of smoked brisket, ribs, turkey, and river trout, plus good vegetables, barbecue sauce, and sensational pies.

LODGING   **Elm Creek Manor,** at 2287 FR 2739 between Muenster and Gainesville (940-759-2100 or 877-356-2733; www.elmcreekmanor.com), a lovely inn sitting on a fourteen-acre spread, combines elements of a vintage New England farmhouse and European architectural pieces. There are six elegant suites, porches, whirlpool tubs, wireless Internet, DVD players, an on-site spa, and amazing food offerings, day and night.

DAY 2/MORNING

BREAKFAST   At your B&B.

Spend the morning catching up on any shopping you didn't finish yesterday, then head west from Denton on US 380 about 6 miles to Farm Road 156, then turn south to the town of Ponder, no more than a wide spot in the road.

LUNCH   **Ranchman's Cafe,** FR 156 in Ponder; (940) 479-2221; www .ranchman.com. This legendary north Texas family spot serves a good, homestyle steak dinner. St. Louis beef is cut in the kitchen only when your order is placed. Baked potatoes are available, too, if you call ahead to reserve the number of spuds your party needs. One last must: Save room for dessert, because Ranchman's is famous for homemade pies and cobblers.

When you've had your fill of lunch, head back to I-35 and home.

There's More . . . .

Denton County Historical Park, with two fine museums, the Bayless-Selby House Museum and the Denton County African American Museum, at the corner of Mulberry and Sycamore Streets in downtown Denton, near the square (www.dentoncounty.com/bsh or www.dentoncounty.com/dcaam). These two museums are part of the park that has plans for two more historic buildings.

Frank Buck Zoo, 1000 W. California St. at I-35, Gainesville; (940) 668-4539. It is home to a camel, a zebra, a red fox, flamingos, llamas, Dorper sheep, goats, aoudad, miniature zebu, red kangaroos, and other beasts.

Special Events & Festivals . . . .

APRIL
Fry Street Fair, Denton; (940) 382-7895. An offbeat festival for alternative music fans, with crafts and food.

Germanfest, Muenster; (940) 759-2227; www.germanfest.com. Three-day festival with wursts, strudels, beer, oompah bands, street dances, barbecue cook-off, arm-wrestling championship, bicycle rally, fun run, and authentic German Mass on Sunday.

MID-AUGUST
North Texas State Fair, Denton; (940) 382-7895. County fair with world-championship rodeo competitions, music, rides, pig races, fiddlers' contest, petting zoo, and barbecue cook-off.

Other Recommended Restaurants & Lodgings . . . . .

DENTON

Sweetwater Grill and Tavern, 115 South Elm St.; (940) 484-2888. Roasted bell peppers and marinated portobello mushrooms raise the level of food sophistication a tad in this favorite watering hole, where the food is as good as the revelry.

GAINESVILLE

Fried Pie Company, 202 W. Main at Commerce; (940) 665-7641. Soups, salads, and sandwiches are fine, but—oh, my—the fried pies are divine.

For More Information . . . .

Denton Convention and Visitors Bureau, 414 Parkway, P.O. Drawer P, Denton, TX 76202; (940) 382-7895; www.discoverdenton.com.

Gainesville Area Chamber of Commerce, 101 South Culbertson St., Gainesville, TX 76240; (940) 665-2831, www.gainesville.tx.us.

EASTBOUND
ESCAPES

EASTBOUND ESCAPE *One*
Canton, Tyler, and Kilgore (By Car)
TREASURES AND ROSES/2 NIGHTS

> Antiques
> Country drives
> Zoo
> Barbecue
> Spring flowers
> Campy museums

Here's an ideal escape for small-town enthusiasts and anybody who likes a good buy. Toss in old-fashioned friendliness, historical surroundings, and a thick forest, and you have an easy, perfect east Texas retreat.

Canton is known far and wide for its First Monday Trade Days, dating back 150 years. The tradition began as farmers and their families came to town the first Monday of each month, which coincided with sessions of the circuit judge. Folks came to sit in on court, gossip and socialize, trade livestock, and buy basic goods to take back to the farm. Today you'll find the custom is a massive swap meet that takes place the full weekend preceding the first Monday of each month. Canton's First Monday grounds cover more than one hundred acres to accommodate 3,000 dealers of antiques, collectibles, and new goods; on a pretty weekend there are 200,000 buyers and sellers.

Athens, meanwhile, is known as the place where the hamburger was created. The story, argued by some, is that Fletcher Davis is the person who first made the American favorite, doing so more than one hundred years ago in a cafe on the Henderson County Courthouse square. There's also some debate about whether the town is named for the Greek capital or the Georgia town; whatever the case, it's popular today for food and antiques.

Tyler, although founded in 1847, had its growth surge during the east Texas oil boom in the 1930s. Most well known today for its

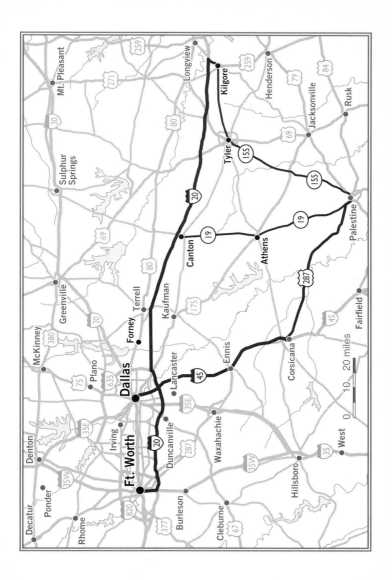

blooms, Tyler is a major rose supplier and a springtime magnet for people on azalea tours.

Kilgore's your destination for exploring the oil-boom days of years past, and for taking in one of the truly marvelous kitschy museums in the state.

DAY 1/MORNING

Get an early start and drive east from Dallas/Fort Worth on I-20 directly to Canton; it's about an hour from Dallas and an hour and a half from Fort Worth.

BREAKFAST **Donna's Kitchen,** 3600 Gus Thomason Rd. in Mesquite; (972) 613-3651. Before you even leave the Dallas metro area, here's a place with an informal, country feel that gets you ready for the real thing. Go for fortifying waffles and sausage, or an omelet, hash browns, and biscuits.

As you head out of Dalla/Fort Worth, keep an eye out for the town of Forney. If you're serious about antiques, you already know Forney. If you want to become an antiques hound, this is a must-stop. Lining either side of US 80 are dozens of antiques stores, both wholesale and retail, constituting a boom of such proportions since its start in 1969 that in 1987 the state legislature designated Forney the "Antique Capital of Texas." Choose from an impressive selection of both American and European antiques. For details contact the **Forney Chamber of Commerce,** P. O. Box 570, Forney, TX 75126 (972-564-2233; www.forneychamber.com).

Then make tracks to Canton for **First Monday Trade Days,** on TX 64 (903-567-6556; www.firstmondaycanton.com). Arrive early to find a parking spot on the square or nearby, then just walk the block east to the expansive fairgrounds. Plan to spend at least a day wandering through what seems like miles of every kind of goods on Earth; you'll see new and old stuff, from oak toilet seats and painted pottery to Queen Anne dining tables and sideboards and antique wheelchairs.

LUNCH Food vendors are set up throughout the trade grounds; choose from burgers, barbecue, sausages, pastries, fresh-roasted peanuts, burritos, lemonade, and soda pop.

AFTERNOON

Continue sifting through the goods: There's every sort of musical instrument, gun, new and used piece of clothing, jelly and jam, pickled vegetable, and video and record you've ever heard of—and lots you haven't. There's kitschy junk to put in the yard, collectible campaign stuff to add to your walls, and plenty of good antique glassware, china, iron beds, quilts, and other furnishings. And the livestock trading of yesteryear continues in the form of puppies (pedigreed and otherwise), rabbits, and guinea pigs. Whether or not you're in the market for anything, it's an experience not to be missed.

If you're ready for a change of scenery, drive down to Athens, about 30 miles directly south of Canton on TX 19.

Your thirst for antiques will be sated in the wealth of shops in Athens, many of which are found at the **Alley Antiques & Collectibles,** a wonderful row of antiques shops just off the northwest corner of the Henderson County Courthouse square, at 400 North Prairieville St. (903-675-9292). There are great buys on large European and early Texan pieces, as well as smaller goods in glass, crystal, and such.

While you're roaming around the courthouse area, look for a historical marker next to the 1927 First National Bank building on the north side of the square. It briefly says that this was the site where a cafe owner named Fletcher Davis (1864–1944) created the first hamburger sandwich in the late 1880s. He exhibited his invention at the 1904 St. Louis World's Fair, in fact. Family members and local friends, as well as the resources of the McDonald's Hamburger University, say the legend is fact.

While you're in Athens, be sure to visit **Texas Freshwater Fisheries Center** 5550 Flat Creek Rd. (903-676-2277; www.tpwd.state .tx.us). Administered by the state parks and wildlife department, the contemporary complex offers 300,000 gallons of aquarium exhibits and the chance to see just about every species of fish found in the state's fresh waters. Habitats include a Hill Country stream, an east Texas farm pond, and a natural wetlands, home to an alligator.

DINNER **The Jalapeño Tree,** 1112 East Tyler St., Athens; (903) 677-4056; www.jalapenotree.com. A mini-chain with locations around East Texas, this upstart brings lively Tex-Mex flavor to town. Appetizers include a layered Mexican dip, quesadillas, and cheesy tortilla soup, and you can choose from among several salads and plates of enchiladas, tacos, and grilled specialties for entrees.

LODGING **Canton Square Bed & Breakfast,** 133 South Buffalo St., Canton; (800) 704-8769 or (903) 567-1680; www.cantonsquarebnb.com. An 1893 Victorian home on the courthouse square has been converted to an inn with five guest rooms. Furnished with antiques, the B&B is within walking distance of First Monday.

DAY 2/MORNING

BREAKFAST At the B&B.

If the weather's warm, head over to **Athens Scuba Park** 500 North Murchison St., Athens (903-675-5762; www.athensscubapark .com) for a morning dive. The owners are devoted scuba divers who decided to build their dream dive site. Spring-fed waters mean there's a visibility beneath the lake's surface of 35 to 70 feet; in all it's 20 to 35 feet deep with a dozen docks onshore and underwater sites to explore that include country singer Ray Price's tour bus, Clint Eastwood's houseboat, and a Lockheed C-140 Jetstar airliner. A well-appointed bath house and full-service dive shop are on-site.

Whatever the time of year, you'll want to see the **East Texas Arboretum and Botanical Society** 1601 Patterson Rd., Athens (903-675-5630; www.eastexasarboretum.org), a 100-acre spread of native Texas flora. Nature decorates 2 miles of hiking trails, and you can see live honeybees (don't worry, they're enclosed) at work. The **Wofford House Museum** is this farmland's window to the past.

From Athens, follow Highway 31 just 36 miles east to Tyler.

LUNCH **Stanley's Famous Pit Bar-B-Q** (525 South Beckham Ave., Tyler; 903-593-0311; www.stanleyspitbbq.com) stands as one of the oldest eating destinations in Tyler and remains a favorite among those who know really good barbecue. The pulled pork sandwich is a big hit, but the Brother-in-Law sandwich scores high points, too, for its combination of chopped beef, hot links, and cheese. You'll like the hickory- and pecan-smoked beef brisket, pork ribs, turkey, and sausage, too.

AFTERNOON

The Tyler Museum of Art (1300 South Mahon Ave., Tyler; 903-595-1001; www.tylermuseum.org) is a great place to while away a leisurely afternoon. With a collection built on 19th- and 20th-century art, the museum also offers exhibitions of work by emerging contemporary artists from Texas and the region. But you never know—you could catch an exhibit of British teapots from the Norwich Castle Museum in England or a collection of 17th-century Japanese folding screens.

DINNER **Clear Springs Texas Seafood,** 6519 South Broadway Ave., Tyler; (903) 561-0700; www.clearspringscafe.com. Here's a place where you can either eat conscientiously, with dishes such as shrimp cocktail "Baja" or grilled salmon salad, or you can get crazy with a mountain of onion rings alongside grilled shrimp, blackened catfish, catfish étouffée, and big platters of fried fish. Landlubbers can opt for fried chicken or grilled steak in a Dijon-peppercorn sauce.

LODGING **Woldert-Spence Manor,** 611 West Woldert St., Tyler; (903) 533-9057 or (800) 965-3378; www.woldert-spence.com. The 1859 home, built by a German immigrant and civil engineer, has been made into an elegant inn with original stained-glass windows, chandeliers, several porches and fireplaces, and seven guest rooms. A full breakfast is served on antique china.

DAY 3/MORNING

BREAKFAST Enjoy the feast at **Woldert-Spence Manor.**

To see the reason for the huge fuss over Tyler roses, look around the **Municipal Rose Garden,** West Front at Rose Park Drive (903-531-1212; www.texasrosefestival.com). Fourteen acres covered with 500 varieties of roses are impressive, especially in a setting of towering pines, gurgling fountains, pretty ponds, and gazebos. Some 38,000 bushes are on display, peaking in May but remaining colorful through October. A camellia garden and tropical greenhouse are on-site, too, along with a rose museum that houses gowns worn by rose queens crowned in years past.

Make time also to see a top Texas attraction, the **Caldwell Zoo,** Martin Luther King Boulevard, 1 block west of US 69 in Tyler (903-593-0121; www.caldwellzoo.org). Begun in 1938 as a family's menagerie, the excellent, eighty-five-acre zoo is a fine example of barrier-free exhibits. In addition to the elephants, giraffes, monkeys, birds, bears, and alligators, there are native Texas animals, a petting zoo, and an aquarium.

Bid Tyler good-bye and head to Kilgore, about 35 miles east on Texas 31, to see how men like H. L. Hunt made their money. The **East Texas Oil Museum,** Henderson at Ross on the Kilgore College campus (903-983-8295; www.easttexasoilmuseum.com), is a surprisingly interesting place. A working oil rig rises outside the entrance, complete with a 70-foot wooden derrick, steam boiler, rotary table, and draw works from the period. The interior's re-created 1930s boomtown helps you understand the hysteria of the day, when Kilgore's downtown was crowded with more than 1,000 oil wells, and 24 of them were crammed onto one acre, then known as the World's Richest Acre. Excellent exhibits explain various aspects of the oil business so a layperson can understand. Open at 9 a.m. to 5 p.m. Tues through Sat, Apr-Sept (and only until 4 p.m. Oct–Mar) and 2 to 5 p.m. Sun.

Down the block there's a good dose of contrast at the **Rangerette Showcase,** which is also on the campus at 1100 Broadway and Ross, in the Physical Education Complex (903-983-8265; www.kilgore.edu/rangerette_showcase.asp). Ten years after the oil boom began, the drill team was born here when the Kilgore Rangerettes first formed a line for precision kicking and dancing. Red Grange called them "the sweethearts of the nation's gridiron," and they still perform at national football events and parades. They were the first to put showbiz on the field, and sexism be damned, they'll be the last to give up their right to wear itsy-bitsy skirts and little white boots and have red-painted lips.

LUNCH   All this museum-going whets an appetite, easily taken care of at the **Country Tavern,** TX 31 just west of Kilgore; (903) 984-9954. Veterans know this honky-tonk serves some of the state's best pork ribs, piled high on platters and served with potato salad, onions, pickles, and local color.

AFTERNOON

Time to head home. Take US 259 North in Kilgore to I-20, and head west to Dallas/Fort Worth.

There's More . . . .

The 1859 Goodman-LeGrand House and Museum, 624 North Broadway, Tyler; (903) 531-1286. Built in 1859, this graceful antebellum mansion is a city museum that exhibits period furniture as well as 18th-century medical and dental equipment.

Harrold's Model Train Museum, 8103 US 271 North, just outside Loop 323, Tyler; (903) 531-9404. Some 1,400 pieces of rolling stock cover 300 feet of track, with more than 1,300 of the trains in lighted showcases. The collection includes wooden trains, antique pieces, and interesting train paraphernalia. Generally open Wed through Sun, but it's best to call for hours.

Hudnall Planetarium, 1200 South Mahon at Tyler Junior College; (903) 510-2312. Multimedia presentations and monthly star parties.

Special Events & Festivals . . . .

MID-MARCH TO EARLY APRIL
Azalea and Spring Flower Trail, Tyler; www.tylerazaleatrail.com. Home tours and a huge 10K race.

MAY
Beauty and the Beast Bike Race, Tyler; www.tylerbicycleclub.com. Magnificent scenery fills a series of rides, with distances varying from 12 to 64 miles. Sag support, T-shirts, rests stops and a post-ride meal are included.

EARLY OCTOBER
Texas Rose Festival, Tyler; www.texasrosefestival.com. Major event since 1933. Thousands of people come to town for this legendary event, which includes a Queen's Tea, parade, art shows, rose show and much more at the site where hundreds of thousands of commercially grown roses are cultivated.

Other Recommended Restaurants & Lodgings . . . . .

CANTON
Plum Lake Cabins, 9½ miles southwest of Canton on TX 198; (903) 848-1033; www.plumlake.com. Three simple cabins are equipped with queen-size beds, TV/VCR, stereo, microwave, toaster oven, small refrigerator, coffeepot, utensils, and fireplace. Secluded hot tubs are next to each cabin, and the hosts will leave a complimentary bottle of wine.

TYLER

Cox's Grill, 706 West Front St.; (903) 593-8940. Excellent Southern breakfasts and old-fashioned burgers.

Rosevine Inn, 415 South Vine, Tyler; (903) 592-2221; www.rose vine.com. Five rooms and baths; wine and cheese in afternoons, gourmet breakfasts.

For More Information . . . .

Canton Chamber of Commerce, 119 Buffalo St., Canton, TX 75103; (903) 567-2991; www.chambercantontx.com.

Kilgore Chamber of Commerce, 813 North Kilgore St., Suite 104A, Kilgore, TX 75663; (903) 984-5022 or (866) 984-0400; www .kilgorechamber.com.

Tyler Chamber of Commerce, 315 North Broadway, Tyler, TX 75701; (903) 592-1661 or (800) 235-5712; www.tylertexas.com.

EASTBOUND ESCAPE *Two*
Marshall and Caddo Lake (By Car)
HISTORICAL HARRISON COUNTY/2 NIGHTS

M arshall is a sleeping giant: At Texas's secession from the Union in 1861, the east Texas city was among the wealthiest and busiest in the state. A center for the production of saddles, harnesses, clothing, powder, and ammunition for the Confederacy, Marshall became the government center west of the Mississippi after Vicksburg fell.

> Southern heritage
> National and state markers
> Antiques
> Bed-and-breakfasts
> Art museum
> Pottery
> Catfish and country food
> Mysterious lake

More than 150 historical markers are found across the county, which hugs the Louisiana state line. So deep is Marshall's heritage that favorite son and newsman Bill Moyers hosted a popular PBS special titled, "Marshall, Texas, Marshall, Texas," in his series, *A Walk through the Twentieth Century with Bill Moyers.* In and around town are plenty of leisurely diversions, and there are good reasons to stop along the way, too.

But it's likely that most people are drawn to Marshall for its proximity to Caddo Lake, the ancient and most fascinatingly beautiful body of water in Texas. You could easily spend a few weeks wandering this giant lake and never understand it all, but give it a try over the next couple of days.

En route, you'll be stopping in Gladewater, a charming little hamlet guaranteed to make the antiques hunter positively giddy.

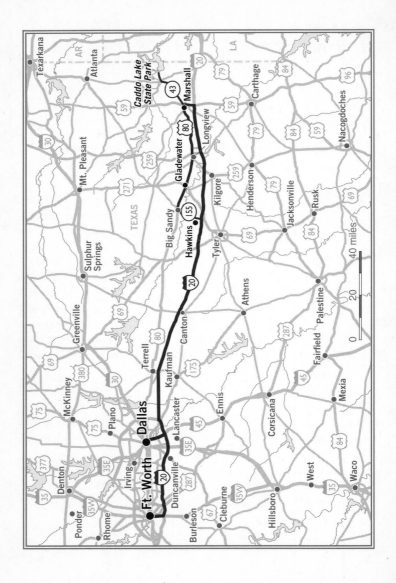

DAY 1/MORNING

Drive east from Dallas/Fort Worth on I-20. Just past Tyler, which is 90 miles east of Dallas, exit onto Farm Road 14 and go north about 12 miles to the minute town of Hawkins. You might have to take a snack to tide you over on the way, but it's worth the wait for breakfast in the town known as the Pancake Capital of Texas. That's because a local woman named Lillian Richards (1893–1956) was selected by the Quaker Oats Company in the early 20th century to portray Aunt Jemima.

BREAKFAST **Jewel's Cafe,** Hawkins, in the middle of town on US 80; (903) 769-4806. Feast on a pile of pancakes or have a platter of eggs, bacon, and biscuits. This charming diner is one of a dying breed.

Continue east along US 80 just 16 miles more to Gladewater, which proudly calls itself the Antiques Capital of East Texas. Once a very rich oil boomtown, Gladewater is now a place that offers excellent deals on antique furniture, dishes and glassware, linens, and assorted knickknacks. In a tiny downtown, there are fourteen antiques malls and fifteen antiques shops, with more than 275 antiques dealers.

In springtime, be sure to visit **Mrs. Lee's Daffodil Garden,** just outside of town (21600 CR 3103, Gladewater; 903-845-5780; www.daffodilgarden.com). A colorful treasure, this 800-acre spread shines a brilliant yellow in Feb and Mar, when millions of blooms cover twenty-eight acres. Walk along 4 miles of trails that wind around two lakes, in woods and valleys, and past a replica pioneer log cabin and three-acre pond.

LUNCH **Guadalupe's Mexican Restaurant,** 208 South Main St., Gladewater; (903) 845-2318. Try the combination plate of tacos, enchiladas, rice, and refried beans. Another option is **Glory Bee Baking Co.,** 111 North Main; (903) 845-2448. The quaint cafe offers soups, salads, sandwiches, and sinful desserts.

AFTERNOON

If you are not in sugar shock, head east on US 80 another 40 miles to Marshall. Stretch your legs and stroll around the **Ginocchio National Historic District,** 612 North Washington. Three square blocks in the old downtown are highlighted by the Ginocchio Hotel, built in 1896. The beautiful Victorian structure, which has been carefully restored and is operating as an Amtrak station, is said to be haunted. Other historic buildings are here, too.

Wander over to the **Harrison County Historical Society Museum,** in the exceptional old county courthouse at Peter Whetstone Square (903-938-2680). Take in the Caddo Indian artifacts, the Civil War and pioneer history exhibits, and the biographical exhibits on famous locals, such as Lady Bird Johnson, Bill Moyers, George Foreman, and Y. A. Tittle. The marvelous old building was completed in 1901 and used continuously as the courthouse until 1964. Its stained glass, domed rotunda, and granite columns are especially beautiful during the winter holiday season when glowing beneath thousands of lights.

Tour the spectacular home called **Maplecroft,** also called the Starr Family Mansion, 407 West Travis St. (903-935-3044; www .tpwd.state.tx.us). It was built in 1870 by James F. Starr, whose father figured prominently in the early years of the Republic of Texas and whose family continued to play critical political and economic roles in the state. The ornate structure and detail are Italianate in design and made entirely of materials shipped from New Orleans. Operated as a state historical park, it's open on Fri, Sat, and Sun only.

Particularly interesting is the **Michelson Museum of Art,** 216 North Bolivar St. (903-935-9480; www.michelsonmuseum.org). Open Tues through Sun afternoons, the 1928 Romanesque building that was once the phone company houses the works of Leo Michelson, one of the late impressionists. Born in Latvia in 1887 and educated in Russia, Michelson lived and worked in Munich, Berlin, Paris, and the United States; his work bears Russian influences as well as those of German and French Impressionism. The collection captures much of his brilliant, seventy-year career.

DINNER **OS2 Restaurant and Pub,** 105 East Houston St., Marshall; (903) 938-7700; www.os2marhall.com. Sitting right on the courthouse square, this Victorian-era building has served over the years as a saloon, billiards parlor, millinery shop, dry-goods store, and Woolworth's Five and Dime. Now it's a gathering spot where you can eat escargot, crab-stuffed shrimp, filet mignon with béarnaise sauce, grilled tuna with lime-butter, and pasta with blackened chicken. And you can once again drink in the saloon and shoot a game of billiards.

LODGING **Three Oaks Bed & Breakfast,** 609 North Washington Ave., Marshall; (903) 935-6777; www.threeoaks-marshall.com. Situated in the heart of the Ginocchio district, this lovely inn is within walking distance of everything downtown. An 1895 historic landmark, Three Oaks offers four big suites with private baths, as well as a wonderful veranda where you can while away the afternoon on a porch swing or in a rocking chair. Big breakfasts are served in the beautiful dining room. Plus, there's wireless Internet connection.

DAY 2/MORNING

BREAKFAST At your B&B.

Before heading to Caddo Lake, stop at a supermarket and stock up for tonight's cookout. You'll need charcoal and lighter fluid, steaks or chicken, potatoes for baking, salad makings, paper plates and paper towels, salt and pepper, salad dressing, butter, and plastic flatware. Ice the perishables in a cheap cooler.

Take US 59 North from Marshall a couple of miles to TX 43; follow 43 about 14 miles and watch for signs to **Caddo Lake State Park,** on FR 2198 in Karnack (see Lodging below). The South's largest natural lake (and the only one in Texas) is a strangely beautiful spread that laps over into Louisiana. Mysterious and magnetic, the 35,400-acre lake is noted for 700-year-old cypress trees, heavily draped with Spanish moss, that stand in and around the water and impart a prehistoric mood. Photographers, painters, and nature lovers are naturally fascinated, but all are well advised to explore these waters with care; the twisting sloughs and canals are profoundly confusing. Guided sightseeing, wildlife-watching, and fishing tours are the best way to go. Ask for information at the state park office; canoe rentals and outfitters are also inside the park.

Look for **Old Port Caddo Rentals and Tours,** inside the state park, 2757 Blairs Landing Rd., Karnack (903-679-3073; www .oldportcaddo.com). Rent canoes, paddles, and life jackets, or book a guided, interpreted boat tour. There's a trading post here, too, selling picnic supplies, bait and tackle, and souvenirs.

LUNCH   **River Bend Restaurant,** 211 Park Road 2422 at Karnack (near the state park); (903) 679-9000. Crab cakes, fried green tomatoes, fried catfish, and pecan pie are among big hits. An appetizer sampler platter consists of, among many things, frogs' legs and fried alligator tail.

AFTERNOON

Take a boat tour or go canoeing in the state park. If the weather won't permit either, take a 13-mile country drive southeast along

Farm Road 134 to **T. C. Lindsey and Company General Store,** in the hamlet of Jonesville (903-687-3382). A family-owned, unpretentious general store in operation since 1847, it's been in Disney movies. There are high ceilings, creaking wooden floors, and shelves stocked with groceries, fabrics, and feed. Off to the side is a room filled with farm tools, hunting traps, horseshoes, etc. Slices from gigantic wheels of yellow cheese plus sodas, chips, and candies offer sustenance until it's time for supper.

DINNER Right outside your rock cabin at Caddo Lake State Park, there's a grill and picnic table. Inside are a stove, sink, and refrigerator. Bake the potatoes, toss a salad, grill the steaks, and eat outside under the stars.

Don't want to cook out at the cabin? Head to **Uncertain General Store & Grill,** Farm Road 2198, Uncertain (903-789-3292; www .uncertaingifts.com/grill). Here's your center of commerce, information, and gossip for Caddo Lake and the greater Uncertain area. You can sign up for paddlewheel boat tours here, book a room at the Uncertain Inn Lakeside, and shop for everything from bait and wineglasses to T-shirts and food. Lunch can consist of pizza, salads, burgers, and fried fish sandwiches to fried gator tail to rib eye steak. Breakfast and supper are served as well.

LODGING **Caddo Lake State Park,** FR 2198, Karnack; (903) 679-3351. The nine cozy cabins are booked up to ninety days in advance, so call ahead; your best bet is a midweek stay. Shaded by towering pines near the water, these cabins offer refreshing, inexpensive escapes.

If the park cabins are booked up, check out small lodgings in Uncertain. These include **Spatterdock** (168 Mossy Brake Rd., Uncertain; 903-789-3268; www.spat terdock.com), a collection of six guesthouses, some rich in history; and **MoonGlow Lodge** (on Taylor Island; 903-789-3940; www.moonglowlodge.com), with three private cabins, all rustic but very comfortable; two with full kitchens.

DAY 3/MORNING

··

BREAKFAST   Whip up some eggs and bacon at your cabin or cottage, or mosey over to **Shady Glade** in Uncertain (903-789-3295). Breakfast is offered lakeside.

Start back home, but set aside at least one hour for a stop at **Marshall Pottery,** on FR 31/Elysian Fields Road just south of US 59 in Marshall (903-938-9201; www.marshallpotterystore.com). Begun in 1895, the pottery is the world's largest manufacturer of red clay pots, making eight million annually. See master potters at work and watch artists paint designs. Also find candles, baskets, dinnerware, linens, glassware, kitchen goods, plants, and silk flowers at huge savings. The enormous yard contains dirt-cheap "seconds" pottery—glazed and unfinished terra-cotta—with tiny nicks, cracks, or flaws.

LUNCH   **Blue Frog Grill,** 101 West Austin St.; (903) 923-9500. Across the street from the newly renovated 1901 Harrison County Courthouse in downtown Marshall.

AFTERNOON

··

After lunch, it's time to head home. Stay on US 59 South to I-20, then head west on I-20 to Dallas/Fort Worth.

There's More . . . .

Caddo Steamboat Company, on Caddo Lake in Uncertain; (903) 789-3978 or (888) 325-5459; www.caddolake.com/steamboat .htm. Daily tours of the lake. Call for hours and reservations.

Mossy Brake Art Gallery, on Caddo Lake in Uncertain; (903) 789-3414. Nature and wildlife are featured in watercolors, paintings, photographs, and books. Art classes and workshops are held in the working artists' studio.

Special Events & Festivals . . . .

OCTOBER
Fire Ant Festival, Marshall; (903) 935-7868; www.visitmarshall texas.org. Hundreds of arts and crafts booths, chili cook-off requiring use of one fire ant, parade, fire ant calling.

LATE NOVEMBER-EARLY JANUARY
Wonderland of Lights, Marshall; (903) 935-7868; www.visitmar shalltexas.org. Beautifully restored historic courthouse and square glow with four and a half million lights. A lengthy schedule of events fills the month.

Other Recommended Restaurants & Lodgings . . . . .

CADDO LAKE
Pine Needle Lodge, on the north side of Caddo near Jefferson; (903) 665-2911. Resembling a ranch bunkhouse, this rustic, lakeside cedar lodge offers one-bedroom units with a large kitchen shared by all guests. Canoe rentals are available.

GLADEWATER
Primrose Lane, 116 East Glade Ave.; (903) 845-5922 or (800) 293-0195. Just 1 block from Main Street's antiques shopping, this 1937 home has two guest rooms with private entrances and baths. A full breakfast is included, and guests have twenty-four-hour access to kitchen facilities.

MARSHALL

Central Perks, 211 North Washington Ave.; (903) 934-9902. Inside the Weisman Center downtown. Enjoy an exotic iced tea and tasty tortilla wrap.

Neely's on Grand, 1404 East Grand Ave.; (903) 935-9040. Here's the "Brown Pig Sandwich" spot.

R&R Bakery & Coffee Shop, 115 East Houston St.; (903) 935-9434. Starbucks coffee and good homemade sandwiches.

Wisteria Garden Inn, 215 East Rusk St., Marshall; (903) 938-7611; www.wisteriagarden.com. Beautiful Victorian-period home offers five rooms with private baths, full gourmet breakfast, and easy walking proximity to downtown shopping.

For More Information . . . .

Marshall Convention & Visitors Bureau, 213 West Austin St., Marshall, TX 75671; (903) 935-7868; www.visitmarshalltexas.org.

Jefferson (By Car)

A SOUTHERN RIVERBOAT LANDING/2 NIGHTS

There is an effortless grace about the old bayou town way over in east Texas that simply isn't duplicated elsewhere in the state. A bit of New Orleans flavors Jefferson, as both flourished as river ports in the 19th century. The Texas town is flavored as well with a Southern softness and a good-time, party-loving spirit.

> 19th-century heritage
> Bed-and-breakfast inns
> Antiques shops
> Historic homes
> Restored downtown
> Bayou town simplicity
> Gourmet dining

Texas history is rich in Jefferson, founded around 1840, so plan at the outset to see lots of wonderfully restored homes and buildings. Chances are extremely good that every visitor in Jefferson will sleep in a historic place, and each can be assured of a memorable, luxurious experience in one of the thirty or so bed-and-breakfasts, inns, and guesthouses. Toss in plenty of good antiques hunting and dining, and it's a marvelous escape to the past.

DAY 1/MORNING

From Dallas/Fort Worth drive east on I-20 to Terrell, about 30 miles east of downtown Dallas, where you'll pick up US 80. You'll follow US 80 and then smaller Texas highways all the way to Jefferson. In all, it's about a four-hour drive. Yes, that is longer than most any Quick Escape, but this is one that's well worth the effort to get up early and make the drive. You'll be amply rewarded with relaxation on the other end.

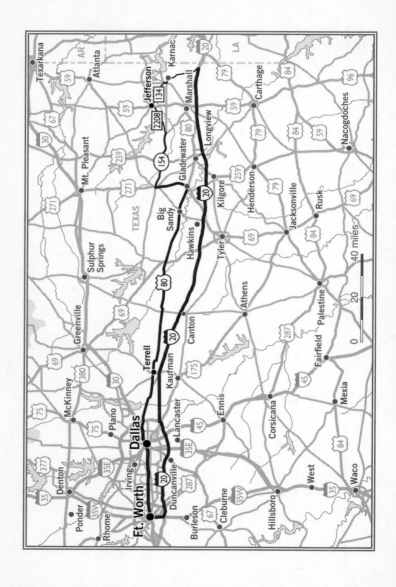

BREAKFAST   There are several small eateries in Terrell. Get a great Mexican breakfast at **Dos Aces,** 304 West Moore Ave.; (972) 524-4446; www.dosaces.com.

From Terrell follow US 80 East through charming little towns such as Mineola and Gladewater. See Gladewater antiques shops information on page 161.

LUNCH   If you want, just tide yourself over with a breakfast bar at home so you can stop for a treat at the **East Texas Burger Company,** 126 East Broad St., Mineola; (903) 569-3140; www.easttexasburger.com. A great place for old-fashioned burgers and chicken-fried steak, it's nothing fancy, but the food's good and the customers are loyal.

AFTERNOON

From Gladewater turn north on US 271 to Gilmer. Next, follow Texas 154 and Farm Road 2208 east to Jefferson. The route courses through pretty, forested land.

The selection of things to do and see in Jefferson (population 2,500) can be a bit overwhelming, but that's a problem remedied by having someone show you around. Check in with the tourism office at **Marion County Chamber of Commerce,** 101 North Polk St., (903-665-2672 or 888-GO RELAX; www.jefferson-texas.com) for a list of tour guides operating this season. You can see the town from aboard a horse-drawn carriage or on horseback, and there are guided walking tours—and even a "ghost walk" tour of haunted sites. Guides deliver colorful accounts of Jefferson's boom days, when it offered one of Texas's original breweries, some 30,000 people lived here, and fifteen steamboats crowded the docks at once.

Another perspective to gain is from the water; **Turning Basin Boat Tours,** US 59 at the Cypress River Bridge (903-665-2222; www.jeffersonbayoutours.com), takes you on the Big Cypress Bayou and provides lore on steamboat days.

To gauge the period's opulence, look around the ***Atalanta,*** 210 West Austin St. (903-665-2513), Jay Gould's private railroad car. Inside are four staterooms, a lounge, dining room, kitchen, butler's pantry, and bathroom. Its presence here is ironic, as financier Gould angrily predicted doom for Jefferson when the city fathers, misjudging the steamboat's future, declined his offer to bring a westward railroad through Jefferson.

Right across the street, the **Excelsior House,** 211 West Austin St. (903-665-2513), is known far and wide for exquisite furnishings and distinguished guests. Rutherford B. Hayes, Ulysses S. Grant, Lyndon B. Johnson (Lady Bird grew up nearby), and Oscar Wilde all spent time here. The 1858 home is available for tours and lodging as well as for a plantation breakfast, by reservation only. This is, in addition to the chamber of commerce office, a good place to ask the locals what's going on in town and who's serving the best piece of pie today.

On the same side of the street, see the big, red **Jefferson Historical Museum,** 223 West Austin St. (903-665-2775; www.jefferson historicalmuseum.com), open daily 9: 30 a.m. to 5 p.m. Local history is told at the old 1888 federal courthouse and post office. Three floors are packed with thousands of artifacts, such as one of the state's finest antique doll collections, a ball gown Lady Bird wore to a state dinner as First Lady, and silverware belonging to Whistler's mother.

Just a block from the museum, the **Carnegie Library,** 301 West Lafayette St. (903-665-8911), built in 1907, is one of three Carnegie libraries still operating in Texas.

DINNER **Lamache's Italian Restaurant,** 124 West Austin St.; (903) 665-6177. Inside the Jefferson Hotel, this restaurant is a reliable source for lasagna and Italian sausage.

LODGING **McKay House,** 306 East Delta St., Jefferson; (800) 468-2627 or (903) 665-7322; www.mckayhouse.com. An antebellum home built in 1851, this exceptional lodging is listed on the National Register of Historic Place and bears a Texas Historic Medallion. The main house has five guest rooms, and the Sunday House Victorian Cottage offers two guest rooms. All have private baths, Victorian-era nightgowns and nightshirts, quilts, exceptional furnishings, and lots of comfort. Several have wood-burning fireplaces. The home itself is beautiful, as are the gardens. The enormous breakfast is served in courses in the dining room.

NIGHTLIFE For a nightcap or a cold beer and nachos anytime, pop into **Auntie Skinner's Riverboat Club,** 107 West Austin St.; (903) 665-7121. The casual, lively spot is friendly.

DAY 2/MORNING

BREAKFAST Should you decide against excellent bed-and-breakfast treats, try the homemade raisin bread done French-toast style at the **Bakery and Restaurant,** 211 North Polk; (903) 665-2253.

You can easily while away the day at the beautifully mysterious **Caddo Lake,** just fifteen minutes to the east via Farm Road 134. Check out the canoe and boat tours in Eastbound Escape Two.

LUNCH **The Hamburger Store,** 101 Market St.; (903) 665-3251. Great burgers and homemade pie are specialties.

AFTERNOON

The historic homes to tour are too numerous for a complete list here. Some good ones to consider are the **Captain's Castle** (1850), 403 East Walker (903-665-2330); **The Grove** (1861), 405 Moseley St., Jefferson (903-665-8018; www.thegrove-jefferson.com); and **House of the Seasons** (1872), 409 South Alley (903-665-8000; www.houseoftheseasons.com). Call for an appointment.

DINNER **Stillwater Inn,** 203 East Broadway; (903) 665-8415; www.stillwaterinn.com. Expect fine things from Bill Stewart, a former Adolphus Hotel (Dallas) chef, such as grilled veal chops, red snapper, soufflés, and good wines.

LODGING **McKay House,** or rent the charming cottage at Stillwater Inn, above. Other excellent choices are found at www.jefferson-texas.com.

DAY 3/MORNING

BREAKFAST Enjoy the morning meal at your bed-and-breakfast or book ahead for the plantation breakfast at the **Excelsior House**. Sit in one of the plush dining rooms and feast on eggs, ham, biscuits, and the hotel's signature orange-blossom muffins.

Mosey around town, checking out antiques shops and boutiques that fill the buildings throughout vintage downtown. The longtime favorite is the **Jefferson General Store** (113 East Austin St.; 903-665-8481; www.jeffersongeneralstore.com), complete with a soda fountain straight from yesteryear. There's 5-cent coffee, too—when was the last time you found that? Great souvenirs include the store-brand black-eyed pea dip, garlic mustard, apricot butter, jalapeño jelly, blackberry preserves, and butter-pecan syrup, as well as T-shirts, toys, and Texas cookbooks.

When you're shopped out, start making your way home by turning westward, but take the scenic route through the land of forested lakes. If you follow TX 49 to Avinger and then TX 155, US 271, and FR 852 to Winnsboro, you'll cross pretty Lake O' The Pines. From Winnsboro, take FR 515 west across Lake Fork to the town of Emory, where you'll pick up TX 276 to follow west across Lake Tawakoni to Quinlan. At Quinlan follow TX 34 south to Terrell; there, pick up I-20 West toward home.

LUNCH   **Lou's Country Inn,** TX 37 South, Winnsboro; (903) 629-7199. A 1908 home transformed into a restaurant, Lou's is a lunchtime favorite for anyone who likes home-cooking. Fresh veggies and salads, corn bread, yeast rolls, desserts made on-site. Look for the slate-blue house with white trim and a shady front porch.

Thus fortified, head west on I-20 for home.

There's More . . . .

City Drug, 109 West Lafayette St., Jefferson; (903) 665-2521. Various gifts.

Texas Treasures, 214 North Polk St., Jefferson; (903) 665-3757. Local souvenirs, wind chimes, home accessories, metal sculptures.

Special Events & Festivals . . . .

LATE FEBRUARY THROUGH EARLY MARCH
Mardi Gras; www.thegrove-jefferson.com. A citywide celebration in grand, New Orleans fashion.

EARLY MAY
Spring Pilgrimage, Spring Pilgrimage, Jefferson; (800) 490-7270; www.theexcelsiorhouse.com/tour. An elaborate tour of homes, whose selection changes each year; and the Diamond Bessie Murder Trial drama.

DECEMBER
Christmas Candlelight Tour; (903) 665-2513; www.historicjefferson foundation.com. Throughout the first two weekends in December, a changing selection of historic homes are decorated in period finery and lighted by candles for your inspection. Candlelight Christmas music concerts, theater productions and a parade are offered, as well.

Other Recommended Restaurants & Lodgings . . . . .

JEFFERSON
Five-D Cattle Company, TX 49 in Avinger; (903) 562-1291; www .fivedcattle.com. Open Tues through Sat evenings, this meeting spot 15 miles east of Jefferson serves rib eye steaks, huge grilled pork chops, mesquite-smoked pork loin, all manner of barbecued meats, hamburger steak, and homemade fruit cobblers.

Jefferson Hotel, 124 West Austin St.; (903) 665-2631; www .historicjeffersonhotel.com. First opened in 1861, this twenty-three-room hotel has recently been renovated. Antiques are mixed with modern amenities.

Old Mulberry Inn, 209 Jefferson St.; (903) 665-1945 or (800) 263-5319; www.jeffersontexasinn.com. The first AAA-approved bed-and-breakfast in Jefferson, this recently constructed inn has five carefully decorated guest rooms with king- or queen-size beds, cable TV, and private baths with antique footed tubs and showers. A member of HAT (Historic and Hospitality Accommodations of Texas), Old Mulberry offers midweek discounts.

Pride House, 409 East Broadway St.; (903) 665-2675. Texas's first bed-and-breakfast in a huge vintage home, lovingly restored. Outstanding breakfast; lovely parlor often used for small weddings. More than ten guest rooms.

For More Information . . . .

Classic Inns Reservations, (800) 468-2627 or (903) 665-3956; www.jeffersontexasbb.com. B&B lodgings can be booked for you.

Marion County Chamber of Commerce, 101 North Polk St., Jefferson, TX 75657; (903) 665-2672 or (888) 467-3529; www.jefferson-texas.com.

WESTBOUND *ESCAPES*

WESTBOUND ESCAPE *One*
Granbury and Glen Rose (By Car)
RIVERSIDE TOWN SQUARES/2 NIGHTS

Antiques shopping
Tearooms
Bed-and-breakfasts
Opera house and live theater
Historic sites
Dinosaurs
Exotic animals
Festivals
Museums

Too bad every escape isn't as ready-made as this one: Granbury is less than 40 miles southwest of Fort Worth and about 60 miles from Dallas. In terms of restorative qualities, however, the Hood County seat is a far cry from any metropolis.

Settled in 1854, Granbury has a model town square that's listed on the National Register of Historic Places. Lake Granbury, whose waters cut through town, is an 8,700-acre, 30-mile-long impoundment on the Brazos River. Plenty of folks wander down from Dallas/Fort Worth just to spend the day antiques hunting or to see a musical at the ever-popular 1886 Granbury Opera House or the Granbury Live Theater. Plan to stay over and savor some relaxation.

About fifteen minutes beyond Granbury, Glen Rose is the seat of Somervell County and a pretty place where the Paluxy River meets the Brazos. From the 1920s through the 1930s it was a thriving health resort. People came to sanitariums here to take the rejuvenating waters. Today people still come, but now for revitalization of the soul.

They also come to see traces of what was, millions of years ago. Clear evidence that dinosaurs roamed this way is offered at a scenic state park. In addition, animals of the modern world are on view at one of the leading international conservation ranches.

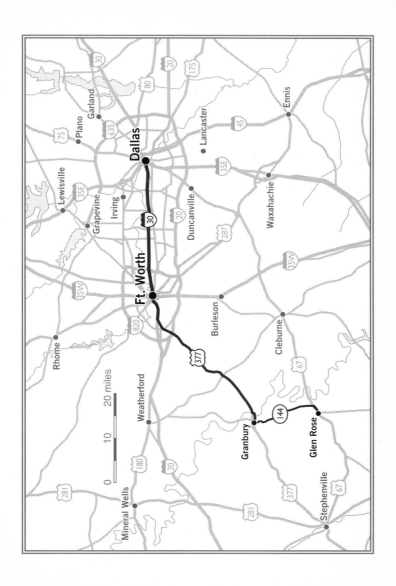

DAY 1/MORNING

··

From Fort Worth drive southwest on US 377 to Granbury; from Dallas, follow I-30 West to Fort Worth, then take US 377 South to Granbury.

BREAKFAST   Stop for a big spread at **Niester's German Restaurant & Deli,** US 377 just east of Granbury; (817) 573-0211. You'll be hard-pressed to find bigger, fluffier pancakes than these, and the eggs with bratwurst are excellent, too.

Just before you reach Granbury, keep an eye out for FR 4; follow it south just 2 miles to **Acton Cemetery.** Inside the pretty country cemetery is **Acton State Historic Site,** a small memorial that honors Elizabeth Crockett, widow of Alamo hero Davy Crockett. She moved to the area after he was killed, but the statue of her, which rises from her gravesite, portrays her with hand to brow, watching and hoping he'll come home to her. During spring, the cemetery and surrounding countryside are covered in blankets of gorgeous bluebonnet.

In Granbury, signs lead to the historic town square. The area fell into disrepair after its 1890s heyday, but a determined local group set about rejuvenating the place in the 1970s. Results are seen on each side of the square in the abundance of charming antiques, book, and clothing shops as well as places to eat and wineries open for touring and tasting.

At the square center is the **Hood County Courthouse,** a cream-colored stone-and-brick creation with its original Seth Thomas clock up top. Off the eastside of the square, the **Hood County Jail,** 208 North Crockett St. (817-578-3537), is the town's jailhouse, crafted in 1885 of hand-hewn stone. After serving its function for ninety years, it became the chamber of commerce; be sure to see the old cell block and hanging tower and pick up touring materials and maps.

LUNCH **Merry Heart Tea Room,** 110 North Houston St. on the courthouse square; (817) 573-3800. Charming room at the rear of an antiques store offers cheese soup, good chicken salad and fruit salad, quiche, and wonderful desserts.

AFTERNOON

Facing the courthouse on the south side of the square, the **Granbury Opera House,** 133 East Pearl St. (817-579-552; www .granburyoperahouse.org), is an 1886 building that serves an enthusiastic theater-going public; productions are usually offered Feb through Dec.

For a treat, have an ice cream or fresh-squeezed lemonade at **Rinky Tink's,** on the west side of the square (817-573-4323), or a huge sugar or chocolate-chip cookie at the **Nutshell Eatery and Bakery** (817-279-8989) on the south side of the square.

Tour the restored **Granbury Historic Railroad Depot,** 109 East Ewell St. (817-573-9246). Built in 1914, it offers a good example of vintage rural Texas train stations.

In fine weather, have a look around the **Granbury Cemetery,** a few blocks north of the square at North Crockett and Moore. Gen. Hiram Granbury, for whom the town is named, and Jesse James are buried here.

History buffs will also enjoy visiting the **U.S. Veteran's Museum** 601 N. Thorp Springs Rd. (817-578-3288; www.usveterans museum.com). Military artifacts come from every war or skirmish involving the United States since the Spanish American War.

The entertainment scene has boomed in Granbury, with such shows as the Branson-styled **Granbury Live,** 110 North Crockett St. on the square (817-573-0303; www.granburylive.com), where the performances offer toe-tapping music from the 1940s through the

1990s. Find programming, which changes weekly, at matinee and evening performances.

DINNER A handful of enjoyable places await you on the square. Two are **Stringfellow's** (101 East Pearl St.; 817-573-6262) offering steaks and chops, as well as a good grilled salmon salad and a lovely patio; and the famous **Babe's Chicken Dinner House** (114 West Pearl St.; 817-573-9777) for fried chicken, chicken-fried steak, pot roast, smoked and fried catfish, veggies and salad, home-made biscuits, and pies—all served family-style.

LODGING **Inn on Lake Granbury,** 205 West Doyle St., Granbury; (877) 573-0046; www.innonlakegranbury.com. Formerly the Doyle House, a historic cottage a couple of blocks from the square and one of the early bed-and-breakfast homes in town, this is now a showplace, thanks to an extraordinary renovation. On a scenic bluff overlooking the lakeshore, rooms at this inn's main house feature a mix of pine, red oak, and maple, as well as elegant linens on a fancy pillow-top mattress, and the baths offer a lovely mix of granite, marble, and tile. The common area has a fireplace, leather couch and chairs, and a help-yourself area with coffee and pastries in the morning and wine and snacks in the afternoon. Five new suites, separate from the main house but also with magnificent lake views, offer contemporary styling, wet bars, fireplaces, and great privacy. Out the backdoor of the main house, in front of the new suites, there's a gorgeous saltwater swimming pool with a waterfall and rock-and-pine landscaping; you can gaze at the lake from poolside, or walk down the live oak-shaded lawn to a boat dock. An elaborate breakfast, served in a large, detached dining room, typically includes a pancake casserole with sausage and maple syrup, Southwestern hominy, eggs with chives, fresh fruit, thick-cut bacon, and blueberry cobbler.

If you have the energy, see what's showing at the **Brazos Drive-In Theater,** 1800 West Pearl St. (817-573-1311). The authentic 1950s drive-in is one of a handful in Texas that still offers outdoor movies.

DAY 2/MORNING

BREAKFAST   Feast on the breakfast spread at the **Inn on Lake Granbury**. Otherwise, see if the brunch buffet is on at the **Nutt House Restaurant,** 119 East Bridge St., Granbury; (817) 279-8688.

Continue from Granbury, leaving US 377 to travel south on TX 144. Within 17 miles you'll reach Glen Rose. Plan to spend a few hours at **Dinosaur Valley State Park,** 4 miles west of town on Farm Road 205 (254-897-4588; www.tpwd.state.tx.us). Experts say these dinosaur tracks are the world's best preserved. Seen in the solid limestone bed of the Paluxy River just above its confluence with the Brazos, the enormous prints were made by the sauropod, a gargantuan creature that ate plants, measured longer than 55 feet, and weighed more than thirty tons. Tracks elsewhere in the region have indicated that the duck-billed dinosaur and the theropod also lived in this area. Near the river, a fenced-off area contains two life-size models of the *T. rex* (*Tyrannosaurus rex*) and the brontosaurus, fiberglass models left over from the Sinclair Oil Corporation's dinosaur exhibit at the 1964–65 New York World's Fair. There is a dinosaur exhibit at the visitor center, too. In addition to displays on everyone's favorite prehistoric creature, the 1,500-acre park has an appealing, shrubby terrain of bluffs and water, ideal for picnicking, camping, and hiking.

LUNCH   **Riverhouse Grill,** 210 Southwest Barnard St., just off the town square; (254) 898-8514; www.theriverhousegrill.net. The handsome Milam House, dating from the very early 1900s, has been beautifully renovated and reopened as a bistro. Specialties include tortilla soup, a portobello sandwich with smoked mozzarella, and grilled salmon with chipotle butter.

AFTERNOON

Continue your dinosaur explorations. Visit the new **Dinosaur World,** 1058 Park Road 59, Glen Rose (254-898-1526; www.dinoworld .net). Perhaps like a Jurassic Park without all the running for your life, this park exhibits 100 life-size dinosaur models in a land-scaped setting, complete with interpretive signs. Kids can do a fossil dig, too, and there are museum exhibits indoors, as well.

Or you can spend the rest of the day at the widely respected **Fossil Rim Wildlife Ranch,** 3 miles southwest of Glen Rose via US 67 (254-897-2960 or 254-897-4967; www.fossilrim.com). More than 1,000 endangered animals from five continents have a 3,000-acre conservation center home here. Along a 9-mile driving tour through the ranch, see such animals as the white rhino, cheetah, gray zebra, and wildebeest roaming around. The scenic overlook halfway through the tour is an excellent place for photos and reflection. The ranch also has a nature store, restaurant, nature hiking trail, riding stables, petting pasture, picnic area with playground, fossil hunting, red wolf and ocelot viewing areas, and guided walks on request. Fossil Rim staffers work with universities, wildlife parks, and zoos around the globe for the purposes of research and training. Special services include educational camps and adult programs; special events such as a wolf howl and a moonlight safari are scheduled.

DINNER **Rough Creek Lodge,** about 9 miles south of Glen Rose via US 67 and CR 2013; (800) 864-4705; www.roughcreek.com. A beautiful dining room awaits inside the main building of a bird-hunting retreat at Chalk Mountain Ranch. An inspired menu offers everything from pheasant and quail to beef tenderloin, sea bass, and plum shortcake. There is also luxurious lodging, tennis courts, a swimming pool, a fitness center, and a sporting clays center on-site. Note that in summer, there are very attractive family packages at the lodge.

LODGING If not at Rough Creek Lodge, above, try **Inn on the River,** 206 Barnard St.; (254) 897-2101 or (254) 897-2929; www.innontheriver.com. The elaborately renovated and decorated twenty-two-room bed-and-breakfast lodge occupies a vintage sanitarium with a state historical marker. Built in 1919, the inn backs up to the serene Paluxy River, a romantic place to weekend and a perfect place to sit quietly and watch the river trickle beneath aged live oaks. Gourmet breakfasts and dinners are offered to guests, and sometimes to nonguests by reservation only.

EVENING

There's still more dinosaur culture to explore. *Land of the Dinosaurs* is a musical show that features massive, robotic dinosaurs, along with a cast of human actors. Performances are offered at 8 p.m., Thurs through Sun, during summer months at the Texas Amphitheater, 202 Bo Gibbs Blvd. in Glen Rose; (254) 230-9589 or (877) 346-6526; www.landofthedinosaurs.com.

DAY 3/MORNING

BREAKFAST At the **Inn on the River.** In winter, enjoy hot berry cobblers; in summer, cold banana bisque; also eggs Benedict, homemade sausage, and fresh fruit.

Before heading home, consider these two fascinating side trips.

Turn west on TX 220 from Glen Rose and drive 26 miles to Hico, where you can prowl through the **Billy the Kid Museum** on Pecan Street (254-796-4004; www.billythekidmuseum.com) on weekends. Local legend holds that Pat Garrett didn't kill the youthful gunman but that Billy lived to be an old man who died of a heart attack when walking down to the Hico Post Office at age ninety.

Or head 35 miles south of Glen Rose, via TX 144 and TX 6, to Clifton. To explore the Norse community, check out the **Bosque County Memorial Museum,** 301 South Ave. Q in Clifton (254-675-3845; www.bosquemuseum.org); call for hours. A small but informative place, the museum has exhibits that detail the founding and growth of the Norse Capital of Texas. You'll see excellent examples of *rosemaling,* the Norwegian craft of painting or carving intricate floral details on all sorts of wooden furnishings. The museum exhibits guns, fossils, coins, tools, and items from pioneer kitchens.

Find out more about the area's bit of Norwegian heritage on a drive into what's known as Norse Country along FR 219 West from town and FR 182 North from town. The Norse settlement was established in the midst of thick juniper by pioneers such as Cleng Peerson and Ole Canuteson in the 1850s. Traditions alive today include a giant smorgasbord at the church in November, when Norse women wear colorful costumes called *drakts.* The Norse church, **Our Savior's Lutheran Church,** on FR 182 about 3 miles north of FR 219 (254-675-3962), sits alone in the countryside and is really special. See Peerson's grave in the churchyard cemetery. For a Norse Country tour, make an appointment with Dan and Mary Orbeck, 403 South Ave. J, Clifton (254-675-8733).

If you're hungry for a great lunch before heading home, stop in **Hico at the Koffee Kup** (TX 6 at US 281; 254-796-4839; www.koffeekupfamilyrestaurant.com) for a burger and slice of their heavenly pie.

There's More . . . .

Fishing on Lake Granbury. Bring your boat and try these waters, where records include 23.5-pound channel catfish, 18.58-pound striper, and 8.68-pound largemouth bass. Ask for details at the visitor center.

Fossil Rim Wildlife Ranch offers the **Foothills Safari Camp,** a different kind of wildlife safari that provides guests with posh tents and full meals. For inquiries and reservations call (254) 897-3398.

The Promise. This passion play, staged during warmer months, may be a response to the dinosaur craze and the evolution theories it suggests. The outdoor musical drama offers a reenactment of the life of Jesus of Nazareth on Fri and Sat evenings, Sept through Oct with a cast of eighty in the Texas Amphitheater (254-897-4341; http://thepromiseglenrose.com).

Special Events & Festivals . . . .

GRANBURY
EARLY MARCH
General Granbury's Birthday and Bean and Rib Cook-off; (817) 573-5299; www.granburysquare.com. The town founder's birthday is honored with a pair of cook-offs, guaranteed to have you on a diet by Monday.

JUNE
Granbury Wine Walk; (970) 389-4017; www.granburywinewalk .com. A weekend of celebration focuses on wines produced in the region. Art events, food-and-wine pairing events and live music add to the appeal.

OCTOBER
Harvest Moon Festival; (817) 573-5299; www.granburysquare .com. A tractor parade kicks off the weekend of playtime, with

attractions including a children's decorated pumpkin contest, kids' play area, antique engine and tractor show, carnival, pooch parade, pumpkin cooking contest, hot dog-eating contest, and pie-eating contest.

DECEMBER
Granbury Candlelight Tour of Homes; (817) 573-5299; www.gran bury.org. Historic homes and commercial buildings are decorated in holiday lights and finery for touring.

Other Recommended Restaurants & Lodgings . . . . .

GRANBURY
The Hilton Garden Inn, 635 East Pearl St.; (817) 579-3800; www .granburyhgi.com. On the Boardwalk along Lake Granbury, 106 rooms.

Iron Horse Inn, 616 Thorp Springs Rd.; (817) 579-5535; www .theironhorseinn.com. Seven rooms with private bath; gourmet breakfast.

American Heritage House, 225 West Moore St.; (817) 578-3768; www.americanheritagehouse.com.

The Nutshell, 137 East Pearl St.; (817) 279-8989. Anchoring one corner of the town square, the Nutshell is a favorite go-to spot for big hamburgers, tuna salad and buttermilk pie at lunch, and there's a good breakfast menu, too.

The Loft, 115 East Pearl St.; (817) 579-1116; www.theloftgran bury.com. The town's only upscale menu offers starters such as filet mignon-blue cheese bruschetta; entrees such as seared rare tuna and orzo salad; and a good wine list. There's a martini bar on site at this chic hideway, too, found upstairs on the square, above the opera house.

GLEN ROSE

Loco Coyote, US 67, 5 miles south of Glen Rose; (254) 897-2324. Outstanding fried catfish, chicken-fried steak, quesadillas, and berry cobblers are served at a country hideout. Call for directions.

The Ranch House, US 67, south of TX 144; (254) 897-3441. A tiny smokehouse sitting under a spreading canopy of pecan trees, this family place serves beef brisket smoked over a pecan fire with exceptional herbed potato salad, as well as smoked turkey, German sausage, ham, and ribs. Open Thurs through Sun.

3 Rivers Grill, 1618 NE Big Bend Trail, Glen Rose; (254) 898-0001; www.threeriversgr.com. Steaks, fish, and salads are among popular choices.

For More Information . . . .

Glen Rose Convention & Visitors Bureau, P.O. Box 2037, Glen Rose, TX 76043; (254) 897-3081 or (888) 346-6282; www.glen rosetexas.net.

Granbury Visitors Center, 116 West Bridge St., Granbury, TX 76048; (817) 573-5548 or (800) 950-2212; www.granburytx.com.

WESTBOUND ESCAPE *Two*
Weatherford, Albany, and Abilene (By Car)
WANDERING THE WILD WEST/2 NIGHTS

Flea market
Farmers' market
Bed-and-breakfasts
Hiking and rock climbing
Frontier fort ruins
Military heritage
Old cemeteries

Here's a trip that will take you deep into Texas's past and into territory only the bravest souls could tame. Established in 1855 and named for Jefferson Weatherford, a state senator, the Parker County seat had only eight families living in the town in 1856. In 1857, the Butterfield Stage came through, which brought more people and commerce. In 1877, however, the area was still very much frontier, as pioneers warred with Native Americans and hundreds of lives were lost. More than a century later, of course, the atmosphere is far more relaxed.

Albany, nicknamed the Home of the Hereford, is where the favorite cattle breed was introduced in Texas's youth. One of Albany's more famous sons was Edwin Dyess, for whom the Air Force base at Abilene is named. One of its more infamous guests was prisoner John Selman, who later killed gunman John Wesley Hardin in El Paso.

Abilene, the Taylor County seat, is home to Dyess Air Force Base. Established by cattlemen in 1881, the town has grown to include contemporary cultural attractions alongside its Wild West heritage on display. Nearby Buffalo Gap is an old pioneer town, restored to its original glory.

On the way west, you'll pass through Mineral Wells, which has several good reasons to stop. Shutterbugs will want to photograph some of the extraordinary architecture in this town, which became

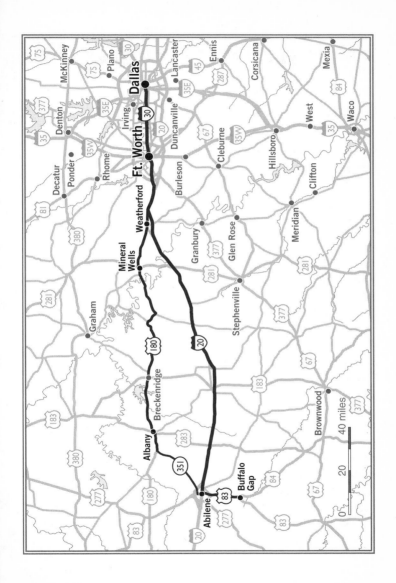

famous in the late 19th century when it was believed that waters from the Crazy Well could cure mental illness and all sorts of other troubles.

DAY 1/MORNING

Weatherford is 20 miles due west of Fort Worth via I-30. From Dallas take I-30 West through Fort Worth, picking up I-20 west of the city. Follow signs to downtown Weatherford.

Stop by the **Weatherford Chamber of Commerce** office, 401 Fort Worth St. (817-596-3801), in the restored Santa Fe depot, built in 1910. Pick up maps of all descriptions; two valuable ones cover Weatherford historic sites by car and by foot. There are guides to dining, lodging, and points of interest, too.

BREAKFAST **Downtown Cafe,** 101 West Church St., Weatherford; (817) 594-8717. Big breakfasts are served daily; choose from a menu of pancakes, French toast, breakfast burritos, biscuits and gravy, and bacon and eggs. Breads are homemade, too.

Stroll around the **Parker County Courthouse,** in the middle of downtown on Fort Worth Street/US 180, the fourth to stand here after its three predecessors burned. This one, made of locally quarried limestone and completed in 1884, is especially Victorian in design, and it costs, interestingly, $55,555.55.

Just 3 blocks east of the courthouse, at Santa Fe and the Fort Worth Highway, **First Monday Trade Days** (817-598-4124) attract thousands of people buying and selling junk, collectibles, antiques, and other stuff. Held the Fri, Sat, and Sun prior to the first Monday of each month, the practice is more than a century old; farmers and ranchers and their families would come to town to do business when court was in session early each month. Today it offers everything, including rabbits, chickens, puppies, and kittens.

Directly across the street, the stucco **Weatherford Public Market** was built in 1932 as a WPA project. Today it's a farmers' market where a colorful cornucopia of fresh produce, flowers, honey, seeds, peanuts, and jelly are sold.

LUNCH **Whistle Hill Cafe,** 104 South Walnut St.; (817) 599-4311. Dine inside or on the porch of this lovely house, which sits high on a bluff, on salads, soups, sandwiches, daily entree specials, and fabulous desserts. Gourmet coffees and cheesecake are specialties.

AFTERNOON

Wander over to the **Weatherford Public Library,** 1014 Charles St. (817- 598-4150), and see the Peter Pan bronze out front. The work of sculptor Ronald Thompson honors Weatherford daughter Mary Martin, who originated the role of Peter Pan in the musical on Broadway. Inside the library's Heritage Gallery, see memorabilia, costumes, photos, sheet music, and other items that belonged to the late actress.

Weatherford's stash of antiques shops is pretty good. Look for shops along Main, York, and Blair Streets. A good place to check out is **Sparks Antiques & Collectibles,** 220 North Main St. (817-598-0089).

Weatherford's driving tour takes in very impressive homes. Just a few to keep in mind include the **Lanham House** at 604 South Alamo, built in 1872; the 1893 Queen Anne beauty at 307 Couts; the beautiful Greek Revival–style Poston home, built in 1908, at 210 South Lamar; and another Queen Anne Victorian at 202 West Oak, famous now as the boyhood home of former U.S. Speaker of the House Jim Wright.

Or take the cemetery tour. Most people search out Oliver Loving's grave, a state historical site in **Greenwood Cemetery,** Front and Mill Streets. His story served as inspiration for novelist Larry McMurtry, who penned the Pulitzer prize–winning novel *Lonesome Dove.* Called the Dean of Texas Trail Drivers, Loving died after being wounded by Native Americans during a trail drive with his friend Charles Goodnight; Loving's son and Goodnight returned his body more than 600 miles to be buried in Weatherford. Other local notables buried in Greenwood include Thomas Snailum, Bose Ikard, J. R. Couts, and Samuel Joseph Redgate.

DINNER **Mesquite Pit,** 1201 Fort Worth Hwy.; (817) 596-7046; www.mesquitepit.com. Mighty popular with the locals, this family place serves mesquite-grilled steaks, burgers, chicken-fried steak, grilled chicken, and smoked barbecue brisket, ham, and pork ribs.

LODGING **Mama's Wish Bed & Breakfast,** 414 West Lee Ave.; (817) 477-4184; www.mamas-wish.com. This renovated 1893 Colonial Revival is said to be the birthplace of Broadway and television star Mary Martin and is located 6 blocks from downtown Weatherford. Four rooms with ceiling fans, swimming pool, deck area, sunroom, and wraparound porch.

DAY 2/MORNING

BREAKFAST A generous spread is served at **Mama's Wish.** The big, three-course breakfast makes a good start before hiking at Lake Mineral Wells State Park.

Lake Mineral Wells State Park, 15 miles west of Weatherford on US 180 (940-328-1171; www.tpwd.state.tx.us), offers rock climbing and hiking around the pretty little lake, but even nonhikers will enjoy the scenery. Swimming, boating, fishing, and picnicking are other possibilities. Paddleboat and canoe rentals are available.

In spring, must-see scenic drives for bluebonnets, primrose, Indian paintbrush, and other wildflowers are along TX 4 South to I-20 and US 281 South to I-20. Both drives begin west of Mineral Wells.

If you're in Weatherford on a Sat or Sun, from Mar through Nov, take time to visit **Chandor Gardens** at 711 West Lee Ave. (817-613-1700; www.chandorgardens.com). This lush, verdant preserve was created by famed English portrait artist Douglas Chandor, for whom such dignitaries as Winston Churchill and Queen Elizabeth sat. Chandor married a Weatherford woman in 1934 and designed their home and exquisite gardens on a hill on the west side of town. Restored and reopened in 1994, the gardens and various features—such as a Chinese pagoda and Japanese water garden—make for lovely, leisurely exploration.

By late morning, head 20 miles to Mineral Wells, a winning town of about 15,000 comfortably nestled in the Palo Pinto Mountains. Weekend warriors are lured to the rock climbing at Lake Mineral Wells State Park and to the canoeing adventures on the nearby Brazos River. On the drive into town, you can't miss the **Baker Hotel,** a magnificent 1929 resort that resembles the Arlington Hotel in Hot Springs. It cost $1.2 million to build and was one of America's most glamorous vacation spots. For twenty-five years people came to take the mineral baths and have various maladies cured, and the famous faces who stayed included Judy Garland, Will Rogers, Clark Gable, and Lord Mountbatten. The Baker closed in the 1960s and hasn't been successfully reopened since then. Still, it's a great subject for photographers. Stop in the **Mineral Wells Chamber of Commerce** at 511 East Hubbard Street and pick up a self-guided tour map. On it you'll find descriptions of twenty-five historic sites, many of which are fabulous buildings that date from 1890.

From Mineral Wells it's another 75 miles west on US 180 to Albany, the seat of Shackleford County. First see the **Old Jail**

Art Center, South 2nd Street near Walnut (325-762-2269; www
.theoldjailartcenter.org). Known as one of the finer small art museums in the Southwest, it's been open since 1980. The storage
vault here is even larger than Fort Worth's esteemed Kimbell Art
Museum. Wings added to the original 1877 structure take nothing
away from its integrity. You can still see the jail keeper's office,
cell, and exercise room, also known as a runaround. Now that area
contains a remarkable pre-Columbian art collection donated by a
Mineral Wells resident. Of note are the Chinese terra-cotta tomb
figures, which date from 206 BC, and a Buddhist prayer book from
Cambodia that dates from the 16th century. Also on display at the
museum are an exceptional jade and amethyst collection, Picasso
drawings, Italian ballroom chairs, and small Henry Moore bronzes.
Look, too, for exquisite furnishings such as the grand piano crafted
from tiger-eye oak in 1895. The museum's courtyard is a pretty
place to pause. Open at 10 a.m. Tues through Sat; at 2 p.m. Sun.

LUNCH　　　　**The Ice House,** 200 South 2nd St. in Albany; (325) 762-
3287. Facing the Old Jail Art Center, this comfortable dining room offers Mexican
fare, burgers, and steaks.

AFTERNOON

Now drive 15 miles north on US 283 to **Fort Griffin State Historical Site,** 1701 N. US 283 (325-762-3592; www.tpwd.state.tx.us),
a 500-acre spread along the Clear Fork of the Brazos River. The
fort dates from the 1867 federal reoccupation of Texas after the
Civil War. Cavalry stationed here fought Kiowa and Comanches and
helped reclaim north Texas. The longhorn is the official animal of
Texas, and the state longhorn herd is based here. Fort Griffin was
on the route where ten million head of Texas longhorns were driven

north to the beef markets a century ago. Nearing extinction around 1920, the longhorn were preserved with help from Western author J. Frank Dobie. The Dobie herd's offspring live at Fort Griffin, while other animals in the state herd live at state parks, including Possum Kingdom, Palo Duro Canyon, and LBJ. University of Texas's mascots, named Bevo, come from Fort Griffin's herd. On the park grounds see a restored bakery, replicas of other fort buildings, and some ruins. There is a fort model and exhibit on fort history inside the visitor center. In addition, there are nature and walking trails, restrooms, showers, a picnic area, and a playground and campsites, some with water and electricity.

The Chisholm Trail's Western Trail split off and came through Fort Griffin, and like Fort Worth, this town was one of the West's wildest, known for gunslingers, gamblers, and outlaws. That's where the *Fort Griffin Fandangle* comes in. The grand outdoor musical has been staged by locals for more than fifty years and is one of the better-known annual events in Texas. Lawlessness, isolation, Native American scares, and the fortitude it took to endure them all are celebrated in song, dance, and pageantry, with longhorns and horses helping to create the mood. Close to a quarter of the townspeople—about 300 people—are involved in the spectacle, which takes place the third and fourth weekends in June.

DINNER   **Fort Griffin General Merchandise Restaurant and Beehive Saloon,** just west of the Albany square on Texas 180; (325) 762-3034; www.fortgriffinandbeehive.com. Chef and co-owner Ali Esfandiary, retired from Dyess Air Force Base and formerly a citizen of Iran, is expert at mesquite grilling tender rib eye steaks and red snapper. A roadhouse from the outside but homey on the inside, with an attached saloon.

LODGING   **Ole Nail House Inn,** on the courthouse square at 357 South 3rd St.; (325) 762-2928 or (800) 245-5163; www.albanytexas.com/nailhoue.htm.

This comfortable bed-and-breakfast occupies the upstairs of a 1914 home whose former resident was Robert Nail, creator of the town's Fandangle. There are ten guest rooms in two houses and two cottages. Breakfast is included.

DAY 3/MORNING

BREAKFAST Breakfast on the sun porch at Ole Nail House usually includes pecan waffles, bacon, and fresh fruit.

Hit the road and drive west 8 miles on TX 6 and south on TX 351 about 40 miles to Abilene. Pick up maps, brochures, and the like at the **Abilene and Forts Trail Visitors Center,** housed in a restored train depot at the corner of North 1st Street and Cypress (625 North 1st St., Abilene; 325-437-2800; www.frontiertexas.com).

Getting a taste of Texas's rough-and-tumble history is a snap at **Frontier Texas!** A state-of-the-art center spreading over several acres in downtown Abilene, this fully interactive destination's high-tech capabilities let you connect with the people who carved a life out of the wilds across the state, putting you inside a herd of stampeding buffalo, a card game gunfight, Indian battles, and scary prairie weather. The perfect jumping-off point for wandering the 700-mile-long Texas Forts Trail, the museum also has a gift store with Texana goods in the way of books, toys, clothes, and home decor.

You can purchase a Roundup Pass for discounts to all Abilene attractions ($15 adults; $7 children). Then walk down the street to see the Museums of Abilene, at **Grace Cultural Center,** 102 Cypress St. (325-673-4587; www.thegracemuseum.org). Open at 10 a.m. to 5 p.m. Tues through Sat and at 1 p.m. Sun. The Children's Museum invites hands-on participation in learning scientific principles, technology's use, and views of everyday life. At the Fine

Arts Museum, exhibits generally include everything from classical to abstract art, using various media. The Historical Museum profiles Abilene's history, from 1900 to 1950, with an emphasis on the recent past.

Next door is the **National Center for Children's Illustrated Literature** exhibiting original artwork of children's books authors and illustrators (102 Cedar St.; 325-673-4596; http://nccil.org)—free and open Tues through Sat 10 a.m. to 4 p.m.

Abilene's military history runs deep beginning with Fort Phantom Hill through WW II and up to the present day with Dyess Air Force Base. Visit the **12th Armored Division Memorial Museum,** 1289 N. 2nd St. in downtown Abilene.

While downtown, visit the Center for Contemporary Arts, art galleries, art studios, catch a movie at the Paramount Theatre, shop till you drop, and find great places to dine.

Abilene's most visited attraction is the **Abilene Zoo** (TX 36 and Loop 322, 325-676-6200; www.abilenetx.com/zoo) featuring over 500 animals, the Creeping Crawler Center, and the popular feeding of a giraffe. Closed only Thanksgiving, Christmas, and New Year's Day.

For fishing or picnicking, head north from Abilene on FR 600 just 10 miles to **Lake Fort Phantom,** covering more than 4,200 acres, with 29 miles of shoreline dotted by marinas, boat ramps, primitive campsites, a swimming beach, and an airfield for model planes. Call (325) 676-6217 for information.

Drive another 4 miles north on FR 600 to **Fort Phantom Hill Ruins.** Great for artists and photographers, the scene is of monolithic, cactus-crowded crumbled masses of stone, as lonely as it must have been 150 years ago. Fort Phantom Hill was established in 1851 as westward settlement activity spread and pioneers fought with the Comanches. It was abandoned in 1854 due to the shortage of water and mysteriously burned soon afterward, yet it was later used as a Texas Rangers outpost and U.S. Army outpost during the 1870s Indian Wars. The ruins are on private property today, but the owner keeps the site open to the public from dawn until dusk.

Or, drive about 6 miles south of Abilene on FR 89 to **Buffalo Gap Historic Village** (325-572-3365; www.buffalogap.com), a popular restored frontier complex, once a stopping place along the famous Dodge City Cattle Trail, that contains nineteen relocated historic buildings such as the Taylor County Courthouse and Jail, circa 1879; a railroad depot that dates from 1881; Abilene's first blacksmith shop; and Buffalo Gap's own Nazarene Church, built in 1902. Souvenirs are available at the trading post.

LUNCH (OR DINNER) **Perini Ranch Steakhouse,** Buffalo Gap; (325) 572-3339. A rustic setting to enjoy Texas eats such as rib eyes with cowboy potatoes and ranch beans, or baby back ribs cooked over mesquite. Call ahead for hours.

You'll be tempted to stay on at **Perini Ranch,** probably to take a two-day nap after your bodacious meal. That's easy, now that Tom and Lisa Perini have opened their Guest Quarters on the ranch, two-tenths of a mile from the steakhouse. The main house is a painstakingly restored 1885 farmhouse that's original to the ranch. Surrounded by rocking, rolling countryside, it's divinely comfortable. Two bedrooms with lavish bedding and beautiful bathrooms, a big living room with a half-bath and high-definition, flat-screen TV, full kitchen with first-rate appliances, dining room, wireless Internet connection, front porch with rockers, and a big deck with fire pit make this a place you'll never want to leave. The second, smaller house has a kitchenette, comfy bedroom, and pretty bathroom. Book at (800) 367-1721 or www.periniranch.com.

AFTERNOON

Time to head back north on FR 89 to I-20, then eastward to Dallas/Fort Worth.

There's More . . . .

Windshield History CD Tales of the Texas Frontier Audio Tour is a program coordinated between Abilene and Fort Worth tourism offices. CD #1 takes you from Fort Worth to Abilene along the Immigrants' Trail, or US 180, and offers interesting tales of the Texas Frontier, and CD #2 takes you back to Fort Worth via I-20. The recordings tell stories of all the towns you'll see along the way. Find them at www.texasstartrading.com.

Lynch Line, 328 South 2nd St., Albany; (325) 762-2212. First edition and other great books, as well as maps and toys, on all things Texana.

Blanton Caldwell Trading Co., 117 South Main St., Albany; (325) 762-2370. Clothing and accessories for women and men, as well as home decor pieces.

Special Events & Festivals . . . .

LATE APRIL
Buffalo Gap Art Festival; (325) 572-3365. In the shade of aged oaks, with art booths, auctions, mariachis, barbershop quartets, and square dancing.

EARLY MAY

Western Heritage Classic, Abilene; (325) 676-2556. Ranch rodeo, campfire cook-off, sheep-dog trials, Cowboy Poet's Society, and Western art show.

JUNE

Parker County Sheriff's Posse Spring Gathering and Ranch Rodeo, Weatherford; www.parkercountysheriffsposse.com/pages/RanchRodeo .htm. A traditional rodeo, starring the famous county sheriff's posse and area cowboys, fills the weekend. There's a chuck-wagon cooking competition, too.

MID-JULY

Parker County Peach Festival, Weatherford; (888) 594-3801; www .peachfestivaltx.com. As many as 30,000 people show up for the one-day party, honoring the juicy, sweet crop abundant in this part of North Texas. The revelry includes a bike ride, dominoes tournament, kids' games and play area, live music, and more than 200 arts-and-crafts booths and food booths.

Other Recommended Restaurants & Lodgings . . . . .

ABILENE

Sayles Ranch, 1001 Sayles Blvd., Abilene; (325) 669-6856; www .saylesranch.com. An enclave of beautifully decorated guesthouses located in one of Abilene's historic districts.

ALBANY

Foreman's Cottage on the Musselman Ranch, FR 601; (325) 762-3576. Three rooms with private baths are within this cottage on a 5,000-acre ranch.

MINERAL WELLS

Nancy's Italian Texan Grill, 2805 US 180; (940) 325-0333. This is a recent favorite among locals and visitors to Mineral Wells. The deep, comforting pasta dishes are highly recommended.

Silk Stocking Row Bed & Breakfast, 415 NW 4th St.; (940) 325-4101; www.silkstockingbb.com. This 1904 Eastlake Queen Anne mansion has five guest rooms and a stocked refrigerator for midnight snacks. Breakfast is served in the main dining room.

For More Information . . . .

Abilene Convention and Visitors Bureau, 1101 North 1st St., Abilene, TX 79604; (325) 676-2556 or (800) 727-7704; www .abilenevisitors.com. **Albany Chamber of Commerce,** Central and Main, Albany, TX 76430; (325) 762-2525; www.albanytexas.com.

Mineral Wells Chamber of Commerce, 511 East Hubbard St., Mineral Wells, TX 76068-1408; (940) 325-2557.

Weatherford Chamber of Commerce, 401 Fort Worth St., Weatherford, TX 76086; (817) 594-3801; www.weatherford-chamber.com.

INDEX